Lockheed SR-71 Blackbird

BOB ARCHER

KEY Books

HISTORIC MILITARY AIRCRAFT SERIES, VOLUME 17

Front cover image: One of the most spectacular sights seen at a UK airshow was the computer glitch that caused fuel to flow into the engines, which momentarily shut down and relit. Huge fireballs were ejected, which briefly hung in the sky as SR-71A 61-7960 displayed at Air Fete '86 on May 24. (Bob Archer)

Title page image: The only SR-71 to feature the 9th SRW emblem on the fin at RAF Mildenhall was 61-7979, which is seen arriving on April 17, 1979. (Paul Bennett)

Contents page image: Tanker pilots' view of SR-71A 61-7980 as Lockheed technicians prepare the aircraft for its sortie on the end of the runway at Mildenhall on March 7, 1986. Interestingly, the aircraft developed a slight technical hitch, and taxied alongside the tanker, affording a bird's-eye view. Soon afterwards, all was well, and the Blackbird launched. (Bob Archer)

Acknowledgements

My first encounter with the SR-71 was in October 1973, when visiting California, I had the opportunity to peek over the perimeter fence at Beale AFB from outside. At some considerable distance away was the row of barns where the Blackbirds were parked, and to my delight, two were open with the tails of an A model and the sole B visible. One year later, the first Blackbird to arrive in the UK landed at Farnborough. Subsequently, I was fortunate to see every one of the 14 that visited the UK during the next 16 years. Much of this text is based upon firsthand viewing obtained through regular visits to Mildenhall, where I was able to watch the aircraft from outside the air base fence.

Many fellow enthusiasts helped with information at the time and subsequently, including Paul Bennett, Paul Crickmore, Glynn Evans, Don Gilham, Colin Johnson, Lindsay Peacock, Chris Pocock, Geoff Rhodes, Chris Russell, Steve Walker, and Dave Wilton. Other friends outside the UK helped with information and photographs, including Joe Cupido, Jim Goodall, Robert Hopkins, and Linda Sheffield Miller. In addition, the enthusiasts' "bible," *British Aviation Review*, provided a wealth of information. I would also like to thank various public affairs officers, especially those at Mildenhall and Edwards AFB, for access to photographs at their bases. Special thanks also to Steve Walker for kindly proofreading the text.

Most of the images are from my own collection, although some of the people mentioned above also contributed. If any of these images are credited incorrectly, I extend my apologies. In particular, the original photographers for the majority of the artworks remain unknown. To these photographers, I extend my eternal gratitude.

Published by Key Books
An imprint of Key Publishing Ltd
PO Box 100
Stamford
Lincs PE19 1XQ

www.keypublishing.com

The right of Bob Archer to be identified as the author of this book has been asserted in accordance with the Copyright, Designs and Patents Act 1988 Sections 77 and 78.

Copyright © Bob Archer, 2022

ISBN 978 1 80282 263 2

All rights reserved. Reproduction in whole or in part in any form whatsoever or by any means is strictly prohibited without the prior permission of the Publisher.

Typeset by SJmagic DESIGN SERVICES, India.

Contents

Introduction 4

Chapter 1   The Blackbird Trio 8

Chapter 2   The SR-71 19

Chapter 3   SR-71 Visits to the UK 36

Chapter 4   Air Fetes, Retirement, and Brief Reactivation 59

Chapter 5   Tail Art, KC-135s, T-38s, and Test vs Operations 69

Appendix 1   SR-71 Deployments to Detachment 1 and 4 83

Appendix 2   First and Last Flights 88

Introduction

The father of the fastest, and arguably the most astonishing, reconnaissance aircraft ever built passed away less than a year after the type was retired for the first time. Clarence "Kelly" Johnson died in Los Angeles on December 21, 1990, not far from his beloved Burbank Skunk Works. The legendary designer probably had more accolades bestowed upon him than any other in the business, and very few visionaries can claim to have been responsible for such cutting-edge technology. His long list of achievements was topped by the SR-71, which was undoubtedly his masterpiece. Designed with the characteristic secrecy that surrounded many of Kelly's projects, the Lockheed SR-71 (and the two predecessors, the A-12 and YF-12 – all affectionately known as Blackbirds) were black projects that eventually emerged into the public arena. Kelly's motto was "be quick, be quiet, and be on time." Well, the SR-71 was very quick, and sorties were always coordinated to be on time, although the third element was way off – the SR-71 being anything but quiet!

On January 18 and 19, 1990, SR-71s 61-7964 and 61-7967 were withdrawn from Detachment 4 at RAF Mildenhall and flown back to the US. Half a world away, the single jet at Kadena Air Base (AB), Okinawa, 61-7962, was returned home on January 21 for the retirement ceremony, which was held at Beale Air Force Base (AFB), California, on January 26. The premature retirement process underlined clearly that the SR-71 program did not have the support at senior levels within the United States Air Force (USAF) that it enjoyed within the corridors of government. And even for the "second coming," when two were revived for service, the USAF did not want it reinstated as operations were expensive,

Kelly's inspiration produced some novel ideas, including the GTD-21 Tagboard reconnaissance drone. The device was carried piggyback-style by an A-12, which was redesignated as the M-21 or "mothership." (via Jim Goodall)

Suitably inscribed with the names of ground technicians, 61-7964 is inside one of the barns at Mildenhall being prepared for the final flight back to the US. (Bob Archer)

Ensuring that everyone in the Mildenhall area clearly understood that the SR-71 operation was at an end, 61-7964 performed a high-speed, very low flyby across the base on January 18, 1990, before heading north for Beale. (Bob Archer)

An unknown SR-71 about to formate on the KC-135 while on a sortie from Beale. (Paul Crickmore collection)

and primarily flown for other organizations, such as the Navy. Therefore, the USAF did everything it could to kill it off. Eventually, President Clinton did just that, with the entire fleet quickly joining museums or other display locations.

Early in the design phase, Skunk Works boss Ben Rich, when he was a young engineer/designer on Kelly's team, suggested that the use of high-grade titanium, which was the primary metal skin, was so difficult to fabricate precisely that a softer version should be used and painted black. The paint would reduce skin temperature through radiation, and significantly ease the incredibly difficult manufacturing process. As the first examples began to emerge from the production line, the aircraft became known as the Blackbird, and retained this nickname throughout the type's lifetime.

During 37 years of flights by the three Blackbird types, the aircraft never ceased to impress everyone who had the privilege to see and hear either a departure, arrival, or a sonic boom as one streaked overhead. Seemingly, the SR-71 even impressed the Russians, as one little-known fact is that during the Strategic Arms Limitation Treaty talks, the Soviet Union representatives openly admitted that there were two American aircraft types that their military feared. One was the General Dynamics F-111, and the other was the SR-71! In the case of the latter, the imagery and electronic data that was acquired was of such importance that, in many instances, the details were presented at briefings given to the president. Without doubt, much of the intelligence was applied to design countermeasures to adversaries' defense posture, to guide senior military and political leaders to allocate budgets to specific areas of defense, and, in several instances, to provide vital details to allied nations that were engaged in conflict. Israel is one such nation whose government benefitted from SR-71 intelligence, which enabled its defense posture to be changed and to overcome attacks by neighboring forces on several occasions.

Introduction

T-38A 64-13271 was one of the first Talons to be stationed at Beale, joining the 4200th SRW before reassignment to the 9th SRW. It is in formation with SR-71A 61-7974. (USAF)

When an SR-71 was relocated to an air base for an airshow, technicians were required to improvise to keep the elements from entering areas such as the engine nacelles. 61-7975 is seen with polythene protection while at a base in the eastern US during September 1985. (Steve Walker collection)

Chapter 1
The Blackbird Trio

61-7979, with the Wing emblem on the fin, taking off from Beale during 1981. (Steve Walker collection)

The Lockheed U-2 was the first high-altitude strategic reconnaissance aircraft, but not long after entering operational service it was considered vulnerable to the emerging surface-to-air missile threat. Therefore, both the Central Intelligence Agency (CIA) and the USAF began thinking about a successor. Whereas the U-2 was subsonic and relied upon its altitude for mission success for invulnerability to air defenses, the general opinion was towards a combination of altitude married to extreme high-speed, and a reduced radar cross section. Lockheed was quick to submit a proposal, allocating the project name Archangel – this being a carryover from the name Angel, which was applied to the U-2 during its development stage.

The proposal was for a capability that was beyond the realms of anything that had gone before. The new requirement was for a reconnaissance asset capable of a cruising speed in excess of Mach 3, with an altitude of 90,000ft, and a range of 4,000nm. The concept of blended surfaces offered a lower radar cross-section, enabling the proposed aircraft to be virtually undetectable by existing radar, and beyond the range of any likely missile threat. The speed alone would defeat all perceived missiles, as their intercept radar sweep would be unable to successfully lock on. In addition to the design matching the requirement, Lockheed also demonstrated that security arrangements were in place, and were rewarded with a contract for the project.

A-12 – the first in line
The designation A-12 was allocated for the first of the family, which was a single seat photographic platform funded by the CIA. The Agency clearly perceived that conventional aircraft designs were no match for the rapidly emerging surface-to-air missile threat. The primary intelligence requirement for

the second half of the 1950s was the dual need to fully understand the level of competency of the Soviet Union nuclear capability, as well as its intercontinental ballistic missile program.

In early 1958, Kelly also understood the necessity when he stated:

> It makes no sense to just take this one or two steps ahead, because we'd be buying only a couple of years before the Russians would be able to nail us again… I want to come up with an airplane that can rule the skies for a decade or more. The higher and faster we can fly, the harder it will be to spot us, much less stop us.

That simple statement was to set the stage for the creations that were to follow.

Brainstorming ideas meant throwing away the rule book and beginning completely afresh. To complete the requirement involved, every facet of the perceived craft had to be completed with radical thinking. Beginning with design number A-1, major changes were introduced until the 12th became the version selected for construction. Everything about the design and manufacture was unprecedented, requiring the most innovative approach to virtually every component.

The proposed new aircraft was to be much larger than the U-2 and with considerably more powerful engines. Possessing a unique shape, with a long, thin fuselage, and blended wings, the conception was as a flying fuel tank, featuring nose-mounted downward and side-facing cameras positioned to capture imagery while flying various profiles. Eventually, the first Oxcart, as the program was known for budgetary purposes, was completed, with the requirement to undertake development and train pilots to fly operationally in secrecy. Therefore, a remote area in Nevada well away from public access was sought, with the site known as both Area 51 and Groom Lake offering the necessary security. Other names applied later included The Area, Dreamland, Paradise Ranch, The Ranch, and Watertown Strip. The abandoned World War Two facilities were upgraded, and the runway resurfaced and lengthened.

A rare image of A-12A 60-6928 at last chance prior to flying a mission from Area 51/Groom Lake. (via Jim Goodall)

A-12 operations were limited to gathering photographic intelligence using wet film. Upon landing at Kadena, the precious film was unloaded and flown by priority aircraft to the Eastman Kodak laboratory in Rochester, New York. Later, a USAF processing plant was opened in Japan to speed up the distribution of photographic intelligence to theater commanders.

Despite the success of the program, the CIA was unhappy to continue funding the A-12, particularly as the SR-71 was becoming operational with the USAF. Whereas the A-12 could achieve higher altitude, and the cameras offered superior resolution, the SR-71 could provide photography as well as electronic and radar intelligence simultaneously.

Left: 456th SAW KC-135Q 58-0054 refueling SR-71A 61-7964 over California during the second half of the 1960s. (via Jim Goodall)

Below: Following their retirement, and prolonged storage, surviving A-12s were allocated for display within museums. 60-6938 is with the USS *Alabama* Battleship Memorial Park at Mobile. (Paul Bigelow)

Under Project Nice Girl, staged between October 20 and November 3, 1967, an A-12 and an SR-71 were flown to determine which would remain in service. Sorties were launched one hour apart over three days and involved flying identical routes supported by aerial refueling. On the first day, the SR-71 completed the task, but the A-12 had a technical problem. On the second day, the reverse was the case. But, on day three, both aircraft successfully flew the route. The weather was low cloud for much of the northern leg, from California to Kentucky, and the A-12 could only photograph cloud cover. However, the SR-71 was able to collect Electronic Intelligence (ELINT) as well as Sideways-Looking Radar data. After air refueling, both Blackbirds accelerated and climbed over the Gulf of Mexico, and from New Orleans to the San Francisco area, the weather was clear, permitting both aircraft to demonstrate their full collection capability for evaluation.

While the first two days' sorties were inconclusive, the intelligence gathered by the SR-71 on the third day was determined to be a better overall investment. The additional SR-71 sensors included infrared detectors, side-looking airborne radar, and electronic intelligence recorders, which were necessary for the post-nuclear-strike capability. Therefore, in the same manner as the president had begun A-12 operations, the presidential process ended Oxcart involvement. The final two A-12s left Kadena on June 8 and 19, 1968. Oxcart facilities at Kadena were transferred to the USAF for use by the SR-71 detachment. CIA pilot Frank Murray made the final flight of an A-12, 60-6937, on June 21, 1968, from Groom Lake to the storage at Palmdale. The sortie officially closed Oxcart operations.

A-12A 60-6924, stored at Palmdale before being restored and displayed at the airport Air Park. (Jim Goodall collection)

Initially, A-12A 60-6931 was allocated to be displayed with the Minnesota Air National Guard at Minneapolis–St. Paul International Airport. However, in 2007, the aircraft was moved to Central Intelligence Agency headquarters at Langley, Virginia. (via Jim Goodall)

In store at Palmdale for many years, before being wrapped in a protective cocoon and parked outside the Skunk Works, TA-12A 60-6927 was being prepared to move the short distance to the California Science Center in Los Angeles in May 1997. (Jim Simpson)

Production

A total of 15 A-12s were produced, with 60-6927 constructed as a two-seater for training. The aircraft, nicknamed the "Titanium Goose," was the only example that was not painted completely black overall, as the jet retained the less powerful Pratt & Whitney J75 engines in place of the same manufacturer's J58. This was due to the aircraft not being required to conduct sorties at Mach 3+ for any appreciable length of time.

Six were lost in accidents, with the surviving nine retired and placed in store with Lockheed in a hangar at Palmdale. They remained hidden from public view until officially being transferred, on paper, to the inventory of the Military Aircraft Storage and Disposition Center (MASDC) at Davis-Monthan AFB, Tucson, Arizona. All were allocated to MASDC on April 15, 1977, although they remained at Palmdale. The transfer to MASDC control was to enable them to be released to various museums in the US.

The YF-12s spent the majority of their flying career operating from Edwards AFB. 60-6935 is seen flying on May 16, 1965, with an Air Force Systems Command emblem on the tail. (via Jim Goodall)

60-6936 has a large white cross applied to the underside to aid with photography focusing during missile launch tests. (via Jim Goodall)

60-6935 exhibited at Edwards on May 16, 1968. Whereas the SR-71 was protected by a barrier during public display, the YF-12 seemingly did not require such protection. (Geoff Peck)

The YF-12

Despite the A-12 being retired, this was not the end of the story for the version. Three A-12As, serials 60-6934, 60-6935, and 60-6936, were constructed as YF-12As to evaluate the possibility of a Mach 3 interceptor. Assigned the program name Kedlock, and initially designated as the AF-12, the change to YF-12A was made around the same time that 60-6934 flew for the first time on August 7, 1963. Seven sorties were performed over the Eglin AFB, Florida, test range to enable the YF-12 to be evaluated firing missiles against unmanned targets. However, the evaluation did not proceed into production, as the Convair F-106 Delta Dart, the last of the century series, had been ordered in sufficient numbers to cater for defense of the continental US. Furthermore, operating costs for the F-106, as well as earlier interceptor types, were significantly cheaper than the expensive YF-12. Nevertheless, the YF-12 was too valuable an asset to simply retire, with two being officially transferred to the National Aeronautics and Space Administration (NASA) on June 5, 1969. These were employed on a variety of tasks, although one, serial 60-6936, was lost in an accident. 60-6935 continued NASA evaluation duties until November 7, 1979, when it was flown to the National Museum of the US Air Force at Wright-Patterson AFB, Ohio. The rear of the third, 60-6934, was used in a hybrid role to create the unique SR-71C, following the loss of SR-71B 61-7957 in 1968. During the limited assignment to NASA, the aircraft were stationed at Edwards AFB with the Dryden Research Laboratory. Their primary duties were to evaluate aerodynamic and extreme heating phenomena encountered during high Mach cruise.

CIA A-12 60-6937 was retired during June 1968. However, NASA was in need of an extra YF-12, with SR-71A 61-7951 being loaned to it on July 16, 1971. To conceal the fact an SR-71 had been borrowed, the serial was changed to 60-6937, and the new designation YF-12C was allocated. The jet remained with NASA until it returned to USAF control on October 27, 1978, and was flown to Palmdale for store on December 22, 1978.

The familiar Air Force Flight Test Center hangars form a backdrop for YF-12A 60-6934 taking off at Edwards. (via Jim Goodall)

The YF-12A conception was intended for Air Defense Command (ADC) to defend the mainland US from an incoming strategic bomber attack. 60-6934 was evaluated at Edwards, with the ADC emblem applied to the tail. (via Jim Goodall)

The sole YF-12C, 60-6937, was in reality surplus SR-71A 61-7951, which was loaned to NASA and assumed the same serial as a retired YF-12A. It is at Edwards on November 17, 1974. (Ray Leader)

The first six SR-71s were ordered on December 28, 1962, and were intended for evaluation. Four of these were lost in accidents by December 1969, leaving just 61-7951 and -7955 to continue non-operational duties. 61-7951 was loaned to NASA on July 16, 1971, as an extra asset, and its serial was changed to 60-6937, along with designation as a YF-12C, to conceal this fact. It returned to USAF control on October 27, 1978, and flew to Palmdale for store on December 22, 1978. Retired on November 7, 1979, after only 796 flight hours, the aircraft was relocated to the Pima Air Museum, Tucson, Arizona, on January 11, 1991. (Doug Slowiak)

Chapter 2

The SR-71

Having successfully completed the A-12 order for the CIA, the Skunk Works team turned its attention to creating a similar design exclusively for the USAF. The primary function was to carry out post-strike reconnaissance following a nuclear exchange. Despite the unlikely possibility of such a mission taking place, the capability was nevertheless required.

Initially designated as the Reconnaissance Strike 71 (RS-71), President Johnson referred to the new aircraft as the SR-71. Not wishing to potentially antagonize the president by stating that he had been given incorrect details, Lockheed decided instead to change the designation on all documentation – not an easy process, as there were millions of references to be altered! For decades, the story was circulated that the president had made the error, whereas in reality the mistake was made by the stenographer, who transposed the letters during the process of preparing the speech.

The SR-71 was a combination of its two predecessors, as the appearance and role were similar to the A-12 but featured the two seats of the YF-12, the rear being occupied by the Reconnaissance Systems Officer (RSO). While the CIA imposed a level of security that was acceptable and manageable to Kelly and his small team, the USAF was different and required tiers of supervising protection to watch over every sector and all levels.

Experience building the A-12s enabled the SR-71 to be produced with fewer of the faults and delays encountered earlier. The biggest change was that, while security was paramount, the aircraft was within the public domain almost from the very beginning of the program. Furthermore, the Blackbird joined the USAF with assignment to a recognized Command and a familiar unit structure. Nevertheless, the SR-71 was initially managed as a black program by Lockheed. On October 29, 1964, 61-7950 was secretly delivered in sections by road from Burbank to Palmdale, just 55 miles to the north. The aircraft was quickly assembled and prepared for its maiden flight. Kelly Johnson received an early Christmas present on Wednesday, December 23, 1964, when the first SR-71A successfully took to the skies over California. With legendary pilot Bob Gilliland at the controls, the sortie from Palmdale was the culmination of an enormous effort by the Skunk Works team at Burbank to ready the aircraft that would spearhead strategic reconnaissance for the next 25 years. A further 30 were constructed,

To ensure secrecy throughout the early period of production, all SR-71s traveled by truck, dismantled and packed inside large wooden crates. The road journey from Burbank to Palmdale was only 55 miles, although the wide load encountered several hazards that needed to be overcome. (Lockheed)

with the final airframe taking to the air for the first time on September 25, 1967. Production equated to one aircraft completed every month by skilled engineers who hand-crafted each component. This was primarily due to the majority of the airframe being forged from titanium, which was an extremely difficult metal to fashion.

Because the president had announced the existence of the new aircraft during his re-election campaign, there was no requirement for the SR-71 program to operate from Groom Lake. Instead, a joint USAF/Lockheed facility was created at Edwards AFB, where the evaluation could take place without the need to completely hide the aircraft from all public view. The first six SR-71As were retained by Lockheed or at Edwards for development. Furthermore, the USAF established the 4200th Strategic Reconnaissance Wing (SRW) at Beale AFB, California, on January 1, 1965, to prepare for SR-71 initial operations. All aircrew selected to transition to the program were initially screened during sorties performed using the Northrop T-38A Talon.

The first two T-38As joined the unit on July 7, 1965. Delivery of the initial Blackbird to Beale commenced on January 7, 1966, when SR-71B 61-7957 completed the short flight from Palmdale. The first SR-71A was flown to Beale on May 10, 1966, believed to be 61-7958. Others followed, with new aircrew being certified as proficient and combat rated.

T-38A 64-13240 had joined the 9th SRW during the late 1970s, and is seen visiting NAS Dallas, Texas, during July 1980, wearing only a Strategic Air Command (SAC) emblem on the fin. The aircraft was still stationed at Beale more than 40 years later. (Peter Wilson)

To commemorate the 1,000th sortie of SR-71B 61-7956, a ceremony was staged at Beale in January 1982. The aircraft accumulated 3,760 flight hours prior to being loaned to NASA, and according to Christy Kincaid at the Kalamazoo Air Zoo Science Experience, the jet finally accumulated 3,967½ hours upon retirement. (USAF)

Far East Operations

Although the SR-71 was ostensibly designed to operate close to the borders of the Soviet Union, the surge in hostile activities across Southeast Asia, and primarily North Vietnam, was the main focus for the majority of early operational missions. The CIA expertise in monitoring North Vietnamese actions was passed on to the Air Force.

The USAF was anxious to employ the SR-71 operationally, as the expensive system was not producing any tangible returns on the investment while operating training sorties at Beale. The establishment of the CIA operation at Kadena provided the facilities necessary for the USAF to begin the undertaking with comparative ease, as the full infrastructure was already in place. The first of three SR-71s, 61-7978, was deployed to Kadena on March 8, 1968, followed soon afterwards by 61-7974 and 61-7976.

Various organizations were formed to coordinate SR-71s at Kadena, beginning with Operating Location 8 (OL-8), before changing to OL-RK (Ryuku Islands) on October 30, 1970. The latter became OL-KA (Kadena) on October 21, 1971, and finally changed to Detachment 1 in August 1974.

Operational SR-71 missions began on March 21, 1968, when 61-7976 flew a 5hr sortie over North Vietnam. The initial flight spearheaded a routine, which was carried out across the nation regularly until 1975, when the North Vietnamese finally swept across the South and brought to an end more than a dozen years of conflict. Throughout seven years of Blackbird operations, numerous surface-to-air missiles were fired, but none found its target. However, as Vietnam ceased to be of interest, the traditional adversaries of China, North Korea and the Soviet Union ensured that Kadena SR-71s remained at the forefront, with regular intelligence gathering sorties adjacent to these adversaries.

An early image of 61-7974, which was one of the first SR-71s to be deployed to Kadena, arriving on March 3, 1968. Decorated with a Habu snake and *Ichi Ban* on the tail, along with 12 small snake mission symbols aft of the cockpit, this image is dated to circa August 1968. "Ichi Ban" in Japanese means "number one in a series." (USAF)

SR-71A 61-7975 about to aerial refuel from a KC-135 while on a flight from Beale. (Paul Crickmore collection)

The thoroughbred Blackbird occasionally developed technical issues that required the pilot to land as soon as practicable. In the case of sorties over North Korea, there were several occasions when an aircraft diverted to USAF bases in South Korea. Usually, the aircraft was soon repaired and flown back to Kadena. However, when 61-7967 diverted to Osan AB on December 11, 1978, personnel from Detachment 2 flying the U-2 took the opportunity to "zap" the SR-71 tail. The detachment's "Black Cats" emblem was applied to the port fin, changing the 1 (for Detachment 1) to a 10, while the starboard side had a zero added. Along the fuselage was the inscription "For Sale – .69 cents." Apparently, the Lockheed technicians were unimpressed when the jet returned to Kadena on December 13.

The SR-71 did not perform any overflights of China or the Soviet landmass, but instead flew peripheral sorties from the relative safety of the Pacific Ocean. Nevertheless, the speed of the aircraft was such that the slightest navigational error could have had a catastrophic outcome, permitting adversaries to maximize their air defense efforts to bring the aircraft down. Hundreds of sorties were flown until the end of 1989, when funding was withdrawn for the sole Kadena aircraft. In preparation to return to the US, 61-7962 flew a number of functional check flights, before departing on January 21, 1990, for the ferry flight back to Beale. A total of 18 different SR-71s were flown from Kadena during 22 years of operations.

Above left: Osan Air Base (AB), South Korea, was occasionally the diversion base when an SR-71 overflying North Korea developed technical problems. The personnel of Detachment 2 took the opportunity to embellish the defective jet before it returned to Kadena. (via Jim Goodall)

Above right: The Detachment 1 tail marking on 61-7967 has been modified into a "10" with the application of the Detachment 2 "Black Cats" emblem. (via Jim Goodall)

Detachment 1 at Kadena decorated the tails of its final aircraft 61-7962 for the retirement sortie on January 21, 1990. Throughout the 22 years of operations from Okinawa, there were many different tail markings, whereas Detachment 4 at Mildenhall had very few. (via Jim Goodall)

RAF Mildenhall, UK

Operating Location-UK was initially responsible for both U-2R and SR-71 operations at Mildenhall, until Detachment 4 was established on March 31, 1979. The sole SR-71A in residence was initially housed in one of the hangars on the southside of the airfield and towed to an apron prior to each sortie being performed. Early in April 1980, a single dedicated small hangar was constructed, which became occupied for the first time when 61-7976 arrived to take up temporary residence on April 9. The detachment was officially given approval to operate two aircraft from April 5, 1982. However, to enable operations to be conducted more effectively, a second dedicated hangar was constructed, both with front- and rear-opening doors, enabling an aircraft to taxi directly inside at the completion of its mission.

To the casual observers outside of the RAF station perimeter fence, the indication that an SR-71 mission was taking place was the launch of the supporting KC-135Qs up to two hours prior. There were normally five/six KC-135Qs in residence at any one time, with the number of supporting tankers being launched indicating the duration and likely location of the mission. Two was the norm, while three or more was commonplace for lengthy sorties, such as those to the Barents Sea, or the eastern Mediterranean Sea. Despite being outwardly supportive, Spain normally refused to permit the SR-71 to overfly its territory, as did France, which was hostile to almost any US military overflights. Therefore, all sorties to the Mediterranean were required to route across the eastern Bay of Biscay/Atlantic Ocean, through the straits of Gibraltar at subsonic speed, before resuming conventional high Mach to perform the peripheral sortie adjacent to the nation under surveillance.

However, most sorties were to either the Baltic or Barents Seas, which ordinarily involved an aerial refueling above the North Sea shortly after departure. Baltic Sea missions would involve a second tanker pre-positioned close to the area of interest. Barents Sea sorties would also require a North Sea aerial refueling, and, depending upon the tasking, at least two more tankers positioned off the Norwegian coast. The tanker departures from Mildenhall were staggered to enable the SR-71 flight to and from the Barents Sea to meet with its support in a carefully choreographed procedure. Depending upon the time required to remain in the vicinity of the target area, there could well be additional tanker support. Quite naturally, SR-71 missions were so important that a backup tanker was always available and ready to launch to replace one of the mission aircraft if necessary.

The Detachment 4 unit board outside hangar 538 on May 23, 1983, when both the SR-71 and U-2 were in residence. The latter tasking was transferred to RAF Alconbury soon after, when the TR-1As commenced delivery to the 17th RW. (Paul Bigelow)

Early Mildenhall operations began with the jet and support equipment positioned on a remote apron, enabling the entire start procedure to be watched and enjoyed by enthusiasts. 61-7964 is seen in the southwest corner on May 10, 1978. (Lindsay Peacock)

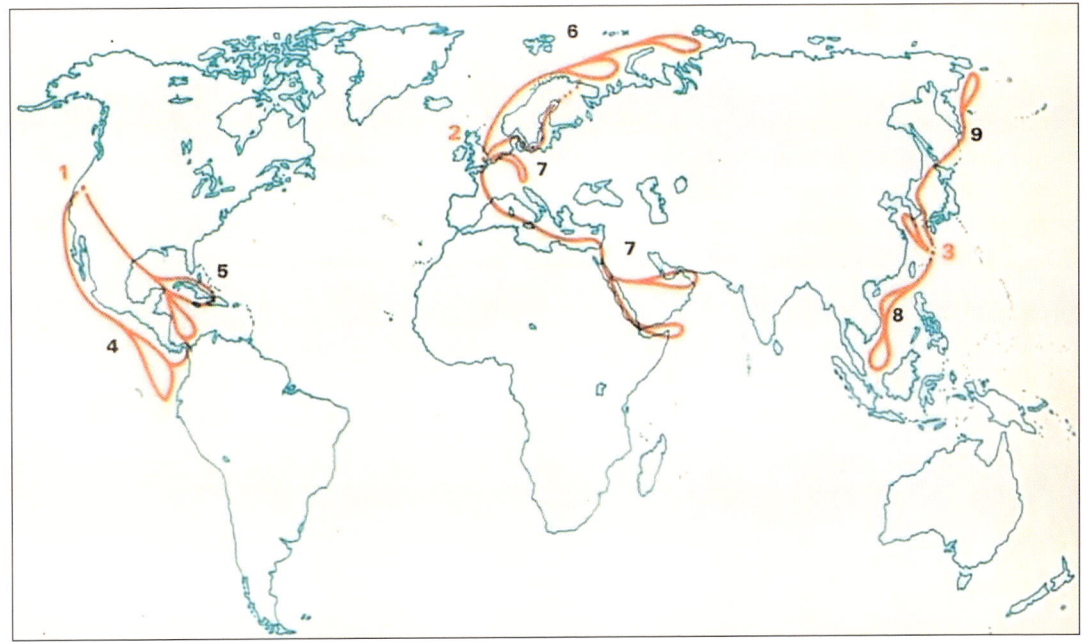

A map prepared during the midpoint of the SR-71's career, depicting the three main operating bases, along with the routes flown to monitor the primary adversaries. SAC's SR-71s flew regularly from three main operating bases, shown in red on the map. 1 was Beale AFB, California; 2 was RAF Mildenhall, UK; and 3 was Kadena AB, Okinawa. The six primary routes are detailed in red and consist of route 4 flights from Beale to Nicaragua and Central America. The Marxist Sandinistas guerrillas were the principal groups of interest on these missions. Route 5 was also flown from Beale to monitor activities in Cuba, as its hostile regime was the nearest to the continental US. Route 6 was to the Soviet Union's Kola Peninsula in the Barents Sea to observe the Northern Fleet. Sorties also flew further into the Soviet Arctic to Novaya Zemlya and beyond. Sorties to the Baltic Sea were occasionally combined also. Route 7 involved sorties along the West German border, as well as through the Mediterranean Sea to the Persian Gulf and Red Sea. All three of these were Mildenhall missions. Route 8 was flown from Kadena to gather intelligence on the large Soviet naval base Cam Ranh Bay, Vietnam, as well as observe activities in North Korea. The final route 9, also launched from Kadena, was to observe activity at the strategically important ballistic missile submarine bases on Sakhalin and Kamchatka, as well as many other military installations in the region. (via Linda Sheffield-Miller)

The primary adversary for the SR-71 was the Russian Mikoyan MiG-25 *Foxbat*. The MiG-25PDs stationed at Finow-Ebberswalde, East Germany, were the principal foe for *Baltic Express* sorties, while other versions, from bases such as Monchegorsk near Murmansk, flew intercept and radar intelligence missions. (Dmitry Pichugin)

SR-71 61-7964 departed Mildenhall during June 1987 for a sortie shortly before the *Baltic Express* incident. A Soviet MiG-25 attempted to intercept it, but armed Danish F-16s prevented it, as did four Swedish Drakens and Viggens. (Bob Archer)

Primary weapons carried by the Soviets interceptors were the Vympel R-33 (NATO reporting name: *AA-9 Amos*), and Molniya R-60 (*AA-8 Aphid*) air-to-air missiles, with the former being especially designed to counter larger airborne US targets such as the North American XB-70 and the SR-71. However, as far as is known, the Russians did not shoot at an SR-71 within the European theater.

Mildenhall SR-71 vs MiG encounter

Due to the speed and altitude of the SR-71, the *Foxbat* was required to fly a pre-determined track to try and reach a similar flight level as the Blackbird. According to Swedish sources, the MiG invariably leveled at 63,000ft, and initially at a distance of 1.6nm astern. On no occasion did the Russian interceptor actually launch any weapons, and it is unlikely that a shoot down would have occurred, because of the defensive systems installed in the Blackbird. From the earliest days of SR-71 operations in Europe, Swedish Air Force air defense radars always tracked the American aircraft, and maintained interceptor aircraft, such as the Saab Viggen, on standby. The Viggens launched periodically for practice interceptions, and to be in a position to shadow the SR-71 if the aircraft inadvertently strayed into their airspace. These opportunities to practice against such a difficult opponent were too good to miss.

On June 29, 1987, SR-71A 61-7964 was on a *Baltic Express* mission from Mildenhall to obtain photographic reconnaissance on a variety of Soviet and Warsaw Pact targets located in East Germany, Poland, Kaliningrad, Lithuania, Latvia and Estonia. The mission was to fly across the Baltic Sea, at a height of approximately 72,000ft, and at a speed of Mach 3.2. The altitude enabled the cameras to see deep into denied territory, while the speed ensured that any attempt to intercept would largely be a fruitless exercise.

While the aircraft was making the initial pass, with the Warsaw Pact nations on the starboard side, one of the engines exploded. The loss of an engine was a requirement to abort the mission, and land at the nearest available safe airfield. Understandably, the Russian Air Force monitored the presence of the SR-71 adjacent to its territory. The SR-71 pilot was unable to maintain either altitude or speed, and therefore made a 180-degree turn to port, to avoid Soviet territory. The Blackbird overflew Gotland Island, thereby violating Swedish airspace. The Swedes immediately launched a pair of JA.37 Viggens from Norrkoping's Airport/AB to assist if necessary. The Viggen pilots determined the SR-71 was experiencing mechanical difficulties and maintained escort formation. Soon afterwards, the two Viggens were replaced by a pair of J.35 Drakens from Angelholm Airport/AB. The Swedes handed the SR-71 over to other NATO air traffic controllers, who vectored the jet to land at Nordholz, West Germany. Danish F-16s and 36th Tactical Fighter Wing (TFW) F-15s from Bitburg AB, West Germany, were also involved in escort duties.

Immediately, a team of Lockheed and USAF technicians were flown to Nordholz in a KC-135Q from Mildenhall to carry out repairs. These were completed on July 2, when the SR-71 returned to Mildenhall. A recently declassified report states the SR-71 landed at Nordholz, which was a sensible alternate as the German Navy flew the Breguet Atlantic in the Signals Intelligence (SIGINT) role from the base. Therefore, Nordholz had the necessary security arrangements in place to safeguard the SR-71 aircraft and intelligence 'take'. Furthermore, the base was in a direct line from the location where the engine fault occurred. However, the flight plan filed for the return of the SR-71 on July 2 was from Stavanger Airport – almost certainly a subterfuge to mask the real situation! The circumstances of the incident were monitored by the Russians in East Germany, who also realized that the SR-71 had deviated from its recognized *Baltic Express* flight profile and launched several MiG-25s. It is widely believed the Russians wished to try and force the SR-71 to land at one of their air bases adjacent to the Baltic, or, if that failed, may even have resorted to shooting the Blackbird down. The Swedes confirmed that at least one MiG-25

Chapter 3
SR-71 Visits to the UK

Throughout almost 16 years of UK operations, there were 14 different SR-71s at Mildenhall. Some were very short-term visits, while others were resident for more than a year. Owing to the complexity of missions flown within the congested airspace in Europe (although no other aircraft except the U-2/TR-1 was likely to be encountered at the operating altitude), only the most experienced crew members were assigned to Detachment 4. The SR-71 was an extremely intricate aircraft to fly, and required crews to rigorously monitor precisely the proximity of the target nations border or territorial waters throughout the mission.

Within the European theater, no aircraft were lost to either an adversary missile or an accident, and despite several malfunctions, often engine related, the pilot always managed to nurse the aircraft back to base or divert to a friendly location. The incredible supporting maintenance personnel were continually ready for such circumstances and able to load a KC-135Q with everything likely to be needed to repair the jet as quickly as possible.

SR-71A 61-7973 departing Mildenhall at Air Fete '87. The diamond shock waves, which were a feature of the J58 engines, are readily apparent. (Darren Currie)

61-7964 landing on January 24, 1981, in the traditional nose-high attitude. Unlike the U-2, which was a glider that defied gravity, the SR-71 was the complete opposite, and dropped like a brick! (Bob Archer)

The sleek SR-71 was an aesthetically beautiful aircraft from almost every angle. 61-7972 lands at Mildenhall on April 18, 1981, a few years before becoming the Skunk Works development aircraft. (Bob Archer)

With spring daisies adorning the grass area, SR-71A 61-7980 returns to Mildenhall at the completion of a mission on June 6, 1983. The jet was the last assignment to Detachment 4, with high visibility markings. 51-7980 spent 1,199 days deployed to Mildenhall. (Bob Archer)

SR-71 spent 5,938 days at Mildenhall during 36 different deployments, with 61-7964 and 61-7972 achieving the most, with six each. The highest total number of days deployed was by 61-7980 with 1,199, while the least was by 61-7958 with just six.

Presented below are the 14 aircraft that staged to the UK, together with some interesting details of their activities.

The ultimate in incognito, SR-71A 61-7955 lands at Mildenhall on July 9, 1983, after a flight from Beale via the Barents and Baltic Sea to evaluate the Loral ASARS-1 operationally. To ensure the subterfuge remained, the aircraft was re-serialed 61-7962, thereby avoiding undue attention. (Bob Archer)

61-7955

- July 9–July 30, 1983. Displayed serial 61-7962 but was really 61-7955.

Clearly the most interesting of all 14 SR-71s that flew from Mildenhall, 61-7955 was the Lockheed development airframe. The aircraft was fitted with the new Loral Advanced Synthetic Aperture Radar System -1 (ASARS-1) high-resolution radar imaging system housed in a detachable nose. ASARS-1 is a real-time, high-resolution reconnaissance system providing all-weather, day-night, long-range mapping capabilities. The system detects and accurately locates stationary and moving ground targets and can survey more than 100,000 square miles of the Earth's surface in one hour. The primary customer was the US Navy, which needed a way to photograph the Soviet Union's ballistic missile submarines as well as the port facilities within the Kola Peninsula.

The new system was such an important improvement that Loral and Lockheed needed to evaluate within an operational environment. The only indication of ASARS-1 being installed on '955 was some minor additional bulges to differentiate from a conventionally shaped nose. Mildenhall was the obvious choice to fly a number of sorties close to the traditional eastern European target area. However, the presence of the Lockheed development aircraft would have undoubtedly created more than the usual passing interest, so maintenance technicians changed the aircraft identity to 61-7962. The subterfuge worked, with the true identity remaining hidden for more than a decade.

61-7955 was flown from Beale to Mildenhall on July 9 completing a Barents and Baltic Seas mission on the ferry flight. On July 18, the ASARS-1 was evaluated again during a 2.6hr operational sortie to the periphery of East Germany. Another, 4hr sortie was flown on July 21, before the aircraft returned to Beale AFB on July 30. The ferry flight to the US was performed with one more evaluation adjacent to the Baltic and Barents, ahead of routing over the North Pole back to California. The operational test worked as required, and soon after returning home the ASARS-1 was cleared for installation in active-duty aircraft. Interestingly, '962 (aka '955) was the last to visit Mildenhall displaying serial, national insignia and lettering in full color, as all subsequent SR-71s had these applied in red.

61-7958

- January 7–17, 1977
- May 16–31, 1977
- December 16–21, 1981
- September 9, 1983–June 12, 1984

The aircraft arrived in January 1977 to perform the type's third familiarization and training deployment, designed to ensure crews were accustomed to the difference between stateside missions and those in Europe. Furthermore, the visit was timed to correspond with the inauguration of new President Jimmy Carter. Owing to Carter's pacifist leaning, the US government considered there was a need to reinforce its military commitment to its NATO allies. Two sorties were flown to the usual regions, which SAC considered was sufficient before commencing peripheral intelligence gathering in earnest when the next planned deployment took place. Indeed, it was 61-7958 again that returned four months later. Clearly, the USAF considered that SR-71 operations were going to be a regular feature in Europe, as in the interim, it authorized the transfer to Mildenhall of an MPC housed in two dozen trailers. These were accommodated in the old US Navy hangar at Mildenhall, better known as Building 538.

By the time 61-7958 returned in May 1977, the MPC was in place and ready to begin functioning. A single training sortie was flown, followed by a coordinated reconnaissance mission to the Barents Sea in conjunction with 55th SRW RC-135V Rivet Joint 64-14846, also flying from Mildenhall. The sortie was conducted on May 20 and was unusual as it was classified as Top Secret. This was undoubtedly due to the Russians having issued a NOTAM (Notice to Airmen) that live missile firing was to take place. Furthermore, the air defense of the Murmansk area had been upgraded with the new NPO Almaz S-200 Angara/Vega/Dubna (*SA-5 Gammon*) medium/high altitude surface-to-air missile. Therefore, the mission was extremely risky, but the decision was made to proceed, as both the Rivet Joint and SR-71 would be flying in international airspace. Despite a small technical issue, the crew pressed on, completed the mission as planned, and not only captured a host of Russian Naval intelligence but also much sought-after radar frequency signals data on the *SA-5 Gammon*.

Having successfully completed the short deployment, the SR-71 was towed to the static park for Air Fete '77 on May 29 to be the star exhibit. This was the first time that a Blackbird was in temporary residence at the base at the same time as the airshow. Interestingly, the USAF needed to make a great many preparations prior to the display. Firstly, the jet was positioned behind a roped barrier at sufficient distance to prevent Soviet or Eastern European agents from obtaining any fragments of the titanium. Furthermore, all sensors were removed, and all fuel drained. Incredibly, the fuselage was heat soaked to an ambient temperature to prevent infrared cameras from discovering the secrets of the aircraft's internal structure and systems position.

Even more fascinating, pilot Buz Carpenter stated:

All four deployed crew members were standing near the aircraft answering questions from the crowd when the Russians showed up in numbers. They took numerous regular and infrared photos and some of the Russians even had hidden microphones. They were a sight to see, coming up like a covey of quail. It looked like the Salvation Army had outfitted them. Their dress sense was

The first public airing of a deployed SR-71 at Mildenhall was on May 29, 1977, when 61-7958 was towed from the south side of the base to the static park. To ensure the Soviet contingent from the London embassy could not scrape samples of the titanium, the jet was positioned just slightly out of reach! (Bob Archer)

that from a 1930s movie about American mobsters. They were attired in bulky double-breasted suits made from rougher cloth than one normally sees, and all clustered around each other waiting for their leader to act. The head of the Soviet delegation, a former MiG-23 fighter pilot was quite relaxed and talkative in his demeanor and invited John Murphy (RSO) and I to drop in Vladivostok in the Far East as a gesture of peaceful relationship. We just quipped "Please forward that request to our State Department."

Two days later the flight back to Beale took place.

The Christmas period was ordinarily a quiet time for reconnaissance operations in Europe, with even the open-ended RC-135 commitment staging back to the US until early in the New Year. However, an exception to this was the situation in Poland in 1981, which involved the population calling for greater democracy and reforms from the unpopular regime of General Jaruzelski, who imposed martial law on December 12, 1981. 61-7958 was flown from Beale to Mildenhall on December 16, 1981, with a sortie around the Baltic Sea to monitor the situation. Another Baltic mission was flown on December 18, before the third and final flight on December 21, which was carried in combination with a loop across the Barents Sea close to the Murmansk area. 61-7958 was then flown across the Atlantic Ocean to recover into Beale after another ten-hour sortie. This was the shortest deployment, as it lasted just six days.

All operational sorties launched from Mildenhall were supported by KC-135Qs, with the initial aerial refueling taking place over the North Sea. 61-7960 is seen closing on a tanker on May 24, 1986. (Paul Crickmore)

61-7960

- October 29, 1985–January 29, 1987

During the mid-1980s, Colonel Muammar Gaddafi of Libya openly supported various attacks on US personnel across Europe. Offering training facilities as well as financial backing, he single-handedly posed a severe threat to Western democracy. Confrontation seemed the only solution to silence the unpredictable figurehead. A build-up of tanker aircraft at RAF Fairford and Mildenhall took place before the evening of April 15, 1986, when the 20th and 48th Tactical Fighter Wings (TFW) launched EF-111As and F-111Fs, respectively, from RAF Upper Heyford and Lakenheath. Named Operation *El Dorado Canyon*, the mission to strike targets in Libya was only moderately successful, but nevertheless, had the desired effect of silencing Gaddafi. Post-strike photography was carried out by the two Mildenhall-based SR-71s, with both airborne simultaneously. A dual mission was flown on April 16 and the two following days, as cloud cover hampered an effective take until the third occasion. To enable the US to release images of the raid to the media, the choice of cameras selected was restricted to daytime operations and clear weather equipment, mounted in an optical bar/panoramic nose. SR-71s 61-7960 and 61-7980 were the two jets in residence with Detachment 4 at the time.

Images captured on film were taken from the aircraft and processed in the MPC before being loaded aboard C-135C 61-2669, which was the aircraft assigned to the USAF Chief of Staff. The imagery was deemed of such importance that the Chief of Staff himself, General Charles Gabriel, accompanied the precious cargo from Mildenhall back to Washington for dissemination to senior politicians, including President Ronald Reagan. This was the only known occasion when both Detachment 4 aircraft flew together operationally.

The crew of the 61-7960, Lieutenant Colonels Mike Smith (pilot) and Doug Soifer (RSO), were selected to display at Air Fete '86, held on May 24. After a very noisy departure, the aircraft flew to the west to prepare for their short series of flypasts. However, while making a run in from the west, the pilot feared he might possibly infringe the display line. Therefore, he tightened the bank angle and applied reheat as they took the aircraft beyond its 2g maximum. The fuel flowed, but the

61-7980 landing at Mildenhall on April 18, 1986, fitted with a panoramic nose to house an optical barrel camera. The aircraft had completed a successful photographic sortie to Libya to capture details of the damage caused during Operation *El Dorado Canyon* three days earlier. (Bob Archer)

A split second before the image presented on the front cover was taken, 61-7960 produced a massive flame that briefly hung in the sky. The resulting spectacle was unique at any airshow in the UK. (Bob Archer)

computers overrode the ignition system. With vortices streaming, as the g-force lessened, surplus fuel was ejected out of the exhaust. In a split second, the unused fuel was ignited as the reheat cut in, causing 13 fireballs in the sky. This was accompanied by a very loud bang, and it was clear to see that the SR-71A had crossed the crowd line, passing behind the control tower. The flying director asked Roger Hoefling, Air Fete director and commentator, if the aircraft's display should be terminated as a result. However, as the crowd line infringement had been an accident, Roger suggested permitting one final pass and then, over the public address system, asked the 100,000-plus spectators if they agreed. A huge roar of agreement from the crowd clearly indicated that the response was unanimous. Disappointingly for those spectators who asked later for a repeat of the events, it had to be declined on the second day.

Maintenance personnel concluded that Triethylborane (often abbreviated to TEB) had been ejected from its container and ignited the JP-7 fuel, causing an excess of flames to be ejected. The ignited JP7 remained aft of the jet exhaust for a few seconds before dissipating. Understandably, the crew were nicknamed the "Fireball Twins."

61-7960 rolling out at Mildenhall on May 25, 1986, with the huge brake chute extended. (Bob Archer)

Any activity by an SR-71 was guaranteed to generate a great deal of interest by the handful of enthusiasts at Mildenhall. With operations conducted in radio silence, the most obvious clues to a mission were the supporting tankers launching. Departure and return were usually great photographic opportunities. SR-71A 61-7962 taxies on December 6, 1984. (Bob Archer)

61-7962

- September 6–18, 1976
- October 19, 1984–October 23, 1985

NATO had wished to include an SR-71 capability within its large-scale exercises held annually in Europe. Therefore, having confirmed the suitability of Mildenhall as the operating base, SAC deployed 61-7962 to Europe on September 6, 1976, to participate in exercise *Cold Fire '76* in West Germany, and *Teamwork '76* above the North and Norwegian Seas. Despite ostensibly supporting the NATO exercises, the aircraft was flown to the Barents Sea area on September 7 and included a photographic pass adjacent to the Soviet Navy facilities.

Ever since the first SR-71 visit to Midlenhall in September 1974, the aircraft occupied a hangar on the southside of the base. This became more problematical when the open-ended arrangement enabled two aircraft to be in residence at any one time. To ease the difficulty, the USAF constructed a new individual barn, followed by a second, both located in the southwest corner. The second was completed on August 8, 1985, with 61-7962 having the honor of beginning occupancy. The new facilities enabled the aircraft to taxi directly into and out without the necessity of a tow tractor. Furthermore, maintenance could be performed within its own secure area, away from other base activities.

Detachment 4 SR-71 61-7964 taxies towards the barn after a mission on December 27, 1980. Deployed reconnaissance assets at Mildenhall sometimes returned to the US for Christmas and New Year, although at other times operational requirements necessitated that they remained through the festive period. (Bob Archer)

61-7964

- April 24–May 12, 1978
- October 16–November 2, 1978
- December 12, 1980–March 7, 1981
- August 16–November 6, 1981 (arrived from Bodo)
- February 5, 1987–March 3, 1988
- October 5, 1988 (to RAF Lakenheath)–January 18, 1990

There were two deployments during 1978, both performed by 61-7964. The purpose of the first visit was to monitor Warsaw Pact troop movements again. Seemingly, the Russians carried out a spring demobilization whereby, on April 1 each year, one third of conscripts were relinquished from military service. Some of these personnel rotated to strategically important positions during the spring and autumn, as this was not possible during winter months due to the extremely harsh weather conditions. The second 1978 visit was for an identical tasking.

After the initial training/familiarization deployments, the majority of SR-71 sorties from Mildenhall were operational. Furthermore, each ferry flight from Beale to Mildenhall and return, known as a Busy Relay, usually included a Peacetime Aerial Reconnaissance Program (PARPRO) mission to the Barents Sea, and occasionally the Baltic Sea while en route. Other sorties to the Barents were "round robins," whereby the aircraft was flown from Beale and back, involving a ten plus hour flight time.

The flight by 61-7964 on August 12, 1981, was one such round robin mission, planned to fly above the Barents Sea to place the aircraft within a provocative nose-on profile at 80,000ft and 2,200mph, pointing directly towards Murmansk! The profile was to make a slow turn, which would place the jet just 12½ miles from the Russian coast (the international territorial limit was 12 miles). The aircraft was flown in an attitude ideal to obtain radar imagery, before continuing back to Beale. However, while in contact with the tanker off the Norwegian coast, a master warning light illuminated, indicating a potentially serious problem, which required the crew to land as soon as possible.

It was quick decision making by crew members Majors B. C. Thomas and Jay Reid, who communicated through the tankers boom connection to advise that they would divert to Bodo AB. Air Traffic transmissions between the SR-71 and Bodo control tower was interesting to say the least, especially as the US aircraft crew could not confirm to the controller the aircraft type over the frequency! Nevertheless, the SR-71 landed, and was soon surrounded by security. The tanker crew passed to Mildenhall all the relevant information, enabling a recovery operation to be organized by the parent Wing. A repair team with a spare engine and all necessary tooling were dispatched from Beale to Bodo by KC-135Q, along with additional tankers containing sufficient fuel to enable the SR-71 to depart.

The maintenance team duly arrived, and it completed sufficient repairs and preparations for the aircraft to fly to Mildenhall at subsonic speed. On August 16, the SR-71 took off on the undulating runway, which caused quite an oscillation. Nevertheless, the SR-71 safely arrived at Mildenhall two hours later, wearing a hastily applied name, *"The Bododian" Express*, and a small crab/whale caricature stenciled on the tails. The SR-71, having arrived in the UK, was therefore retained by Detachment 4, as one was scheduled to be deployed to Mildenhall soon after anyway.

The remainder of the short stay was uneventful. At the completion of this adventurous deployment, 61-7964 was readied to return to Beale on November 6. Shortly before taxiing, the tail was decorated with a chalk inscription "MAC & Crew" above the serial, and a rectangle containing "FOR SALE" below. Furthermore, the serial on the tail had been altered with chalk from 17964 to 17984, probably

Left: *"The Bododian" Express* tail markings, applied to 61-7964 when the jet diverted to Bodo on August 12, 1981. (via Jim Goodall)

Below: Making an unexpected visit to Mildenhall on August 16, 1981, 61-7964 was to have flown a round robin from Beale to the Barents Sea, but it diverted to Bodo with a technical issue. Following repairs, the jet continued to Mildenhall to assume the commitment to monitor the Eastern Bloc autumn troop rotations. (Bob Archer)

Bottom: *"The Bododian" Express* taxies at Mildenhall in September 1981. (Andy Thomson)

Departing Mildenhall for a Peacetime Aerial Reconnaissance Program (PARPRO) sortie while deploying back to Beale on November 6, 1981, 61-7964 has hastily applied tail art, inscribed "MAC & Crew" above the serial, alongside a rectangle containing "FOR SALE." Note also the serial has been altered from 17964 to 17984 in chalk. (Bob Archer)

an amusing little episode as SAC reconnaissance aircraft periodically had their tail numbers changed. It is more than likely that this graffiti had gone by the time the jet landed at Beale.

61-7964 arrived from Beale again on February 5, 1987, with a small emblem and the inscription "Sky Shark" on the fin. However, these had been removed by the time the aircraft flew its first operational mission next day. During a Barents Sea mission on March 6, 1987, the aircraft suffered an engine fire, and diverted to Nordholz, West Germany. The jet was absent for about 14 days. Another visit to Norway occurred on October 19, with the jet not returning to Mildenhall until three days later.

A very important mission took place on January 16, 1988, with the SR-71 launching in the most appalling weather conditions. Thick fog had descended over Mildenhall when it was time to return, requiring the jet and supporting pair of KC-135Qs to divert to Bentwaters. No details have ever been released as to the purpose or the destination of the sortie.

61-7967 taxiing at Mildenhall, on June 26, 1989, viewed from arguably the most advantageous photographic location outside of the base. Many European sorties commenced at precisely 0800hrs, and returned some four or five hours later, probably indicating a PARPRO to the Baltic Sea. (Bob Archer)

61-7964 arrived for the sixth time in October 1988, landing at Lakenheath as Mildenhall was closed for runway work. After spending 15 months in Europe, and with the program no longer funded, the aircraft was the first of the resident Detachment 4 aircraft to return home. Throughout the entire 16-year period, all activities were surrounded in a veil of secrecy, although the departure on January 18 was conducted in the full glare of publicity. A reasonably sized group of media were permitted access to the individual aircraft barn, to view the Lockheed technicians preparing the jet. With all systems ready, the two crew members arrived and posed for photography ahead of taking their seats and running through the start-up procedure. The aircraft then eased its way out of the barn and taxied to the end of the runway. The media group were relocated to the runway midpoint, to view the very impressive departure, and a single low-level flyby was flown before the aircraft met with the first air refueling. Unbeknown to all present, except a handful of personnel with the necessary clearance, the SR-71 flew to the Barents Sea to perform one last operational sortie, even though funding was not in place. The USAF considered that as the aircraft "was going roughly that way, anyway, it might as well carry out a mission."

The final sortie from Mildenhall was flown by 61-7967 on November 20, 1989, which landed after completing several overshoots. This flight effectively ended operations by Detachment 4. (Bob Archer)

61-7964 leaving Mildenhall for the last time on January 18, 1990, for the flight to Beale. Two months later, the jet was allocated to the Strategic Air Command & Space Museum at Ashland, Nebraska. (Bob Archer)

61-7967

- March 2, 1989–January 19, 1990

The aircraft had the honor of performing the final planned mission with Detachment 4, when the jet flew from Mildenhall on November 20, 1990. At the completion of the flight, the crew performed several overshoots, almost certainly to use up remaining fuel, as well as enjoying the unique aircraft for one last time. Together with Detachment 4 sister aircraft, 61-7964, the two jets flew a test sortie on January 16, 1990. It is not known if the two aircraft flew together while over the North Sea, although this would appear to have been a golden photo opportunity. With all systems functioning as required, the aircraft departed on January 19, and, after a single flypast of the base, turned north to land some hours later at Beale. This symbolic sortie effectively ended Detachment 4 operations, and it closed a most enjoyable and enduring aspect of Mildenhall's illustrious history.

One of the very few occasions when both aircraft were airborne simultaneously was January 16, 1990, for air tests. 61-7967 returned to Mildenhall with the brake chute refusing to release. Ground crew did not like the situation, as one member had to scramble up onto the extremely hot fuselage to "kick" the offending catch and free the mechanism. (Bob Archer)

Spectacular departures were always a feature of an SR-71 sortie, with the diamond shock waves seen here produced by 61-7971 leaving Mildenhall on February 2, 1983. Within a few minutes, the jet would connect with the first of several tankers. Incredibly, the SR-71 was more fuel efficient at high Mach, and therefore required a tanker to assist with the jet attaining altitude. (Bob Archer)

61-7972 lands at Mildenhall during April 1981, when visits were comparatively rare. (Don Gilham)

61-7971

- December 23, 1982–February 2, 1983
- March 13, 1988–February 28, 1989

61-7972

- September 9–13, 1974
- April 20–30, 1976
- March 12–28, 1979
- September 13–November 2, 1980 (some operations from Lakenheath)
- March 6–May 5, 1981
- December 18, 1982–July 6, 1983

61-7972 initiated the SR-71 visitations to Europe during September 1974, as the previous sorties to the region did not land. During the Yom Kippur war in October 1973, plans were made for an SR-71 to depart the US and fly with the aid of aerial refueling to overfly Israel, Syria, and Egypt, before flying back along the entire length of the Mediterranean Sea, and, after passing Portugal, recover into Mildenhall. The sortie would last 8½hrs. However, Prime Minister Edward Heath vetoed the plan, as he was concerned about oil supplies from Arab countries being halted by nations supporting Israel. Therefore, missions were flown to and from the US lasting more than 11hrs. The war ended abruptly when the Israeli military overwhelmed its aggressors, due in no small part to the invaluable details captured by the SR-71. The priceless intelligence, including highly accurate disposition of enemy forces, was promptly passed to the Israelis, who adjusted their battle plans accordingly to win the campaign.

The swift end of the war, combined with the continued oil supplies, persuaded the Heath government to agree to an evaluation of SR-71 for missions from the UK. However, in order to ensure this was carried out without too much suspicion, a plan was devised whereby the aircraft would arrive in a blaze of publicity, capturing speed records in the process. Furthermore, to maximize the exposure, the aircraft was to land on the Sunday preceding the Farnborough International Airshow. On September 1, 1974, 61-7972 departed Beale AFB, crewed by pilot Major James V. Sullivan and RSO Noel F. Widdifeld, and flew across the US before the dash across the Atlantic Ocean. The aircraft crossed the timing gate above New York, and 1hr 54mins and 4secs later passed through the invisible line above London. The distance was 3,461.5 miles, thereby establishing a new trans-Atlantic record, which remains to this day.

The aircraft was displayed to the general public the following weekend when the event was open for three days. At the completion of the airshow, the SR-71 quietly flew to Mildenhall on September 9 to enable the ground evaluation to take place. Departure was scheduled for September 11, although a technical issue forced a two-day delay. The SR-71 did successfully depart, and, with the assistance of

Above: Basking in the traditional late summer sun, wind and rain, SR-71A 61-7972 was the undisputed star of the static park at the 1974 Farnborough International Airshow. (Bob Archer)

Right: The details of the astonishing new speed record from New York to London on September 1, 1974, were displayed alongside SR-71A 61-7972 at Farnborough. (Geoff Rhodes)

air refueling by several pre-positioned KC-135Qs, it flew direct to Beale in a time of 3hrs 47mins and 39secs. Crewed by pilot Captain Harold B. Adams and RSO Captain William C. Machorek, it flew the 5,446.9 miles, and established a new speed record between London and Los Angeles.

The two-day stay at Mildenhall permitted Beale personnel to conduct an investigation of whether the infrastructure was suitable for SR-71 operations. It is believed that the aircraft remained hangared and was not towed or taxied during this short stay. While at Mildenhall, the SR-71 received a complete engine change, which was accomplished by USAF personnel who arrived aboard one of eight KC-135Q flights into Mildenhall.

Ironically, after a gap of 19 months it was 61-7972 that was the first to deploy to the new OL. The visit was planned to fly two training sorties above the North and Norwegian Seas, and the English Channel/Bay of Biscay. The sorties were largely successful and enabled planning to be formulated for future missions in Europe. Subsequently, 61-7972 flew back to Mildenhall for three more short-term, and one long-term, stays. Of these, the deployment on March 12, 1979, was in response to a request from the Saudi Arabian government following tension between North and South Yemen. The South Yemenis were aligned to Marxism, while their northern neighbor was a more moderate government. The Saudi king was concerned with the possibility of the extremist South invading North Yemen, resulting in a fanatical state in the Arabian Peninsula.

61-7972 was flown to Mildenhall and readied for the first of a series of very long missions. After two aborts owing to adverse weather in the target area, the first sortie was launched on March 16.

The Blackbird that initiated European operations. 61-7972 is about to depart Mildenhall on September 12, 1974, having carried out a short evaluation of suitability for the type to fly from the base. However, a minor technical issue delayed departure until the following day. (Bob Archer)

61-7972 was the first SR-71A to visit the UK and was at Mildenhall a further five times. It is seen here taxiing out for a sortie during March 1979. (Andy Thomson)

In customary fashion, the French and Spanish refused the US request to overfly their territory, resulting in the aircraft routing over the Atlantic Ocean, through the Gibraltar Straits, across the Mediterranean Sea, before entering Egyptian airspace. A dash over the Red Sea placed the aircraft precisely in the correct position to make two passes over the North Yemen/Saudi border. Having activated the cameras at precisely the correct time, the crew then reversed course, and retraced their flight back to Mildenhall. The 10hr mission was the first of others that would follow during the subsequent years. At the completion of this hurriedly arranged deployment, the aircraft was flown back to Beale on March 28.

61-7972 was deployed again on September 13, 1980, for the traditional autumn missions. However, during mid-October, the base began runway resurfacing work during normal working hours, resulting in the SR-71 relocating to Lakenheath on October 15 for the remainder of the stay. The aircraft was housed in one of the hardened aircraft shelters (HAS), although it is highly likely that only the forward section could be comfortably accommodated. However, the HAS would have afforded security when sensors and noses were changed.

Above: 61-7972 without the nose attached at Mildenhall on May 4, 1983. Different cameras were installed in these interchangeable noses. (Paul Bigelow)

Right: One of the many functional checks the pilot performed prior to take-off was to ensure the vertical stabilizers swiveled as required. The SR-71 is one of the few aircraft types to feature this characteristic. SR-71A 61-7973 is at Mildenhall on March 21, 1987. (Bob Archer)

The final visit to Detachment 4 by 61-7972 began on December 18, 1982, to replace 61-7974, which had returned home on December 13. However, '972 developed technical issues, resulting in 61-7971 arriving on December 23 to carry out missions. 61-7972 was finally serviceable by January 25, 1983, when the aircraft flew its first operational mission. The resumption to operational status enabled 61-7971 to return to Beale on February 2. This was the first occasion when two SR-71s were with Detachment 4.

61-7973

- November 1, 1986–July 22, 1987

The aircraft was flown during the flying display on May 24 at Mildenhall's Air Fete '87. The SR-71 has quite a low g-force loading, and is reported to have exceeded this number, resulting in the aircraft being grounded. It is believed that Lockheed technicians carried out tests to determine the stress on various sections of the fuselage and wings. A test sortie was carried out on July 17, which obviously confirmed that the jet was safe to perform a single flight from the UK direct to Palmdale on July 22. Interestingly, the ferry flight to the US involved air refueling from KC-135Qs, which were already airborne from Mildenhall to support Detachment 4 sister aircraft 61-7964, which was flying a planned PARPRO mission. This was one of just a handful of occasions when both Mildenhall SR-71s were airborne at the same time.

Above: 61-7973 performing a spirited display at Air Fete '87 on May 24. Unfortunately, the aircraft was overstressed during the demonstration, and it was grounded while an investigation was carried out prior to the granting of a single sortie back to Palmdale. The aircraft did not fly again, and was eventually displayed in Blackbird Airpark, outside the Lockheed plant. (Bob Archer)

Left: With an earth-shattering roar, 61-7974 departs Mildenhall on May 12, 1982. (Lindsay Peacock)

At Palmdale, technicians performed extensive stress level tests, but seemingly the cost to return the aircraft to fully operational status was prohibitive. The aircraft was placed in storage with Lockheed and eventually displayed at Blackbird Airpark at Palmdale.

61-7974

- April 30–December 13, 1982
- August 2, 1983–July 16, 1984

The aircraft made a single divert to Bodo on both of its deployments to the UK. The first was between May 7 and 9 1982, and the second on April 5 and 6, 1984.

Parked in the center of the base at Mildenhall on May 3, 1982, 61-7974 is firmly anchored to the ground, with the aid of long steel poles attached to metal rings set into the concrete. The SR-71 brakes were insufficient to restrain the aircraft when power from the J58 engines was being tested. (Joe Bruch)

61-7975 was only in residence during the summer of 1984, and it is seen flying past RAF Alconbury on July 28. (Bob Archer)

The only SR-71 to display the skunk emblem on the fin while deployed to Mildenhall was 61-7976, which is seen departing on a sortie on October 29, 1977. (Bob Archer)

61-7975

- July 16–October 16, 1984

61-7976

- October 24–November 16, 1977
- October 18–November 13, 1979
- April 9–May 9, 1980

Making the third short-term deployment during 1977, 61-7976 arrived from Beale on October 24. The plan was for the aircraft to fly from Beale to the Barents Sea and conduct a joint sortie with RC-135U Combat Sent 64-14849, which would fly from Mildenhall. At the completion of the mission, both aircraft would recover to the UK. Subsequently, the SR-71 flew eight sorties above West Germany, routing along a dedicated track to minimize engine noise. The track was parallel to the DDR (German Democratic Republic) and Czechoslovakian borders, enabling electronic intelligence and high-resolution radar details of Warsaw Pact troop dispositions to be verified. Shortly after arriving in the UK, the tails were zapped with a white Playboy Bunny motif applied on the starboard side, and a skunk to port.

55th SRW RC-135s were occasionally coordinated to fly a joint sortie, enabling both types to engage in their specialized intelligence gathering missions. RC-135U 64-14849 is seen departing Mildenhall on October 24, 1977, to meet with SR-71 61-7976 above the Barents Sea. (Bob Archer)

On November 16, the SR-71 departed Mildenhall for the ferry flight back to Beale and, for the second time, coordinated activities with RC-135U 64-14849, this time within the Baltic Sea. 61-7976 was the only aircraft at Mildenhall that displayed the Playboy Bunny emblem on the fin.

Left: 61-7976 taxiing at Mildenhall during October 1977, displaying the Playboy Bunny motif on the tail. (Chris Pocock)

Below: The only SR-71 that flew from Mildenhall with the 9th SRW emblem on the tail was 61-7979, which is seen arriving from Beale on April 17, 1979. (Bob Archer)

61-7979

- April 17–May 2, 1979
- June 14, 1984–July 17, 1985

To effectively coordinate activities of both the resident U-2 and the periodic SR-71 deployments, the USAF formed Detachment 4 at Mildenhall on March 31, 1979. The twice-yearly SR-71 visits had taken place primarily to record as much information as possible on the spring and autumn Warsaw Pact troop rotations usually involving Soviet forces being sent to the Iron Curtain nations. 61-7979 was the first SR-71 to be deployed to Mildenhall under the new organization. The aircraft was displaying a full color Wing badge on the tails.

During the second deployment, 61-7979 flew a lengthy Middle Eastern sortie on July 27, 1984, routing through the Straits of Gibraltar owing to the usual French and Spanish refusal to permit an overflight. The sortie was beset with problems, one of which was inlet malfunctions, which required the aircraft to fly slower than the traditional Mach 3+. Ordinarily, the issue would have required the crew to abort the mission, but as the aircraft handled responsively in manual mode, it enabled a single pass to take place over Lebanon, before it commenced the long flight back to Mildenhall.

The slower speed had consumed more fuel than planned, resulting in the SR-71 requiring the tankers orbiting near Crete to urgently fly east. From the lofty altitude, the SR-71 pilot saw the KC-135s below, and performed an extremely sporty descent to level off immediately behind the first tanker. The "take" was declared to be exceptional, which went in favor of the crew who had flown a degraded aircraft within limits of a surface-to-air missile site.

Right: Making a spectacular departure from Fairford on July 16, 1985, 61-7979 displays the characteristic huge flame from the rear of the two J58 engines. (Mike Freer)

Below: Despite technicians meticulously preparing each aircraft for overseas deployments, the complex technology occasionally required rectification in theater. Seen on April 2, 1983, 61-7980 is being towed to a remote area for ground engine runs. (Bob Archer)

61-7980

- January 5–April 27, 1982
- March 7–September 6, 1983
- July 19, 1985–October 29, 1986
- July 27, 1987–October 3, 1988 (from RAF Lakenheath)

When 61-7980 arrived on January 5, 1982, this was the beginning of an almost continual SR-71 presence at Mildenhall. From this date onwards, there was only rarely a time when one was not in residence – usually involving the departing Blackbird returning home before a replacement arrived soon afterwards.

61-7980 is believed to have diverted to a Norwegian base while on a flight from Beale to Mildenhall on March 5, 1983. Four KC-135Qs were launched that day, presumably to refuel the inbound SR-71, but no aircraft arrived in the UK. However, 61-7980 landed at Mildenhall two days later, accompanied by only one KC-135Q, signifying that the jet had diverted.

The fourth assignment to Detachment 4 was as a result of 61-7973 being overstressed in May 1987 when displaying at Mildenhall's Air Fete. 61-7980 arrived on July 27 with an eagle motif on the tail, which had been removed prior to the first operational mission.

61-7980 and fellow Detachment 4 resident 61-7964 were both very active at the end of August 1987, flying long sorties from Mildenhall to the Persian Gulf. They were supported by KC-10As, as well as the usual KC-135Qs, for the missions flown on August 28 and 30. A 380th BW KC-135Q flew from Mildenhall to Andrews AFB and back on August 29 and 31 presumably carrying the photographic details from these two missions.

Left: At Greenham Common airshow in July 1983, 61-7980 was attacked with white paint by peace camp protesters, although ground crew quickly cleaned off the mess. The following day, the aircrew made a "spirited" departure, before aiming the jet at the protestors' nearby camp, and giving them a very low diving pass before applying full afterburner, which blew several tents away! The jet is seen leaving Greenham Common a few minutes earlier. (Bob Archer)

Below: With an entourage of Lockheed and USAF support personnel in trail, SR-71A 61-7958 taxies for a sortie on June 2, 1984. (Bob Archer)

Chapter 4
Air Fetes, Retirement, and Brief Reactivation

Mildenhall's air fetes

The presence of an SR-71 at Mildenhall was initially kept relatively quiet, although the popularity of the aircraft, to both military personnel and civilians in the region, was such that it was inevitable that the type would eventually be shown to the public. The debut was Air Fete '77, when temporary resident 61-7958 was on static display for the May 29 event. The undisputed star was towed from the southside hangar to a position almost within touching distance of the throng that gathered alongside the metal fence. No SR-71s were in residence again until Air Fete '82, staged on May 29 and 30. By this time, Detachment 4 had been formed, with 61-7974 displayed on both days, while its U-2R 68-10337 was outside building 538 on just the first of the two days. This was the only event when the detachment was operating both aircraft.

The SR-71 became a regular feature in both the static and flying program at Air Fetes from May 1984, with 61-7974 debuting to make a highly impressive display. This included an asymmetric flypast with only the starboard afterburner lit, and the pilot countering the power effect with both tails swiveled! Interestingly, the event also featured a British Airways Concorde – both types being unique in operating in afterburner, and at Mach speed as a matter of routine.

Throughout the 1980s, the annual Air Fete at Mildenhall usually had an SR-71 on static display, which was without doubt the primary reason for the massive crowds. 61-7967 is seen parked outside building 538, where the Mobile Processing Center was located. Note the huge Detachment 4 banner draped over the hangar's upper section. (Bob Archer)

61-7967 surrounded on one side by an eager crowd of spectators at Air Fete '89. Note in the background the Detachment 4 sales stand, proudly proclaiming "Home of the Blackbird" and "Skunk Works Souvenirs." Understandably, trade was extremely brisk with the huge Mildenhall crowd eager to buy mementos of their day out. (Bob Archer)

The unique presence of an SR-71 first on static display only, and subsequently within the flying program, was almost certainly one of the reasons why Air Fete attracted such a massive audience. Spectators attending would often relate that the Blackbird was the major draw, followed closely by the availability of the delicious American barbecues and beers. The Blackbird was an unrivalled spectacle at events in Europe, with Mildenhall guaranteed to have one, and sometimes two, on public view.

Closing the door – the first time

Detachment 4 at Mildenhall closed down its operations on January 24, 1990. Following the earlier withdrawal of funding, both aircraft were grounded until December 7 and 8, 1989, when they performed a proficiency sortie ahead of all personnel returning home for Christmas. The two aircraft were safely shut away in their individual barns, before 9th SRW KC-135Q 58-0103 brought the crews and technicians back to Mildenhall on January 12. Both aircraft were prepared for a test flight on January 16, one of only a few such occasions when the pair were both airborne at the same time.

With all arrangements in place, the first SR-71 to depart Mildenhall was 61-7964, crewed by Major Tom McCleary and RSO Lieutenant Colonel Stan Gudmundson, which took off shortly before noon

Pilot Major Tom McCleary and RSO Lieutenant Colonel Stan Gudmundson pose for photography outside the barns at Mildenhall on January 18, 1990, prior to ferrying 61-7964 back to the US. Despite no funding for operations, the crew flew to the traditional Barents Sea area for "one last time," prior to continuing the flight to Beale. (Bob Archer)

To commemorate the 25th anniversary of SR-71 operations on December 22, 1989, a Detachment 4 crew member designed this verse: "To the (with apologies to Pepsi-Cola) Kelly Inspirin', Rich Thinkin', Skunk Workin', J58 Drivin', J.P.7 Burnin', Missile Avoidin', Mig Loosin', High Flyin', Record Settin', Mach Bustin'.... BLACKBIRD." The doggerel was taped to the wall in one of the Detachment 4 offices and was probably thrown away when the unit closed down! (Bob Archer)

on January 18 in glorious sunshine. The following day, 61-7967 departed at the same time as 61-7964 the previous day. 61-7967 was crewed by Major Don Watkins and RSO Bob Fowlkes. Both aircraft performed a low-level flyby before the traditional extremely noisy climb to altitude. KC-135Q 59-1513 supported both departures, with an aerial refueling above the North Sea.

Concurrent with the closure at Mildenhall was an identical situation at Kadena AB, where Detachment 1 SR-71 61-7962 was test flown on January 18, and returned home four days later, flown by pilot Major Steve Grzebiniak and RSO Major Jim Greenwood. The last sortie by the Wing took place at Beale on January 26, when an official ceremony retired the type from service, with senior Lockheed personnel, including Skunk Works boss Ben Rich, in attendance, as well as General John T. Chain, the Commander in Chief of SAC. SR-71A 61-7960 was flown by pilot Lieutenant Colonel Rod Dyckman,

The saddest of moments, the SR-71 decommissioning ceremony at Beale on January 26, 1990. Left to right president of Lockheed's Skunk Works, Ben Rich, SAC/CC General John Chain, RSO Lieutenant Colonel Tom Bergam, pilot Lieutenant Colonel Rod Dyckman, 9th RW commander Colonel James Sarvarda, Lieutenant General J. J. Murphy 15th Air Force/CC, Brigadier General Larry Mitchell 14th Air Division/CC, and one unknown pilot. General Chain was one of the architects of the SR-71's demise, as is evidenced by his smile. Undoubtedly, it is a very poignant moment for Ben Rich, who is clearly upset that the masterpiece he, Kelly, and the team worked so hard to design was being withdrawn. (USAF)

An aerial view of the retirement ceremony at Beale on January 26, 1990. (USAF)

and RSO Lieutenant Colonel Tom Bergam in front of a very emotional gathering. Whereas most present were sad to see the Blackbird program ended, General Chain smiled throughout, as he was one of the prime architects for the demise, and wished the budget to be allocated elsewhere.

As stated, several aircraft were flown to museums and air bases for display. Of particular interest was 61-7972, which latterly served as the flight-test example with Detachment 6, 2762nd Logistics Squadron at Palmdale. The aircraft was earmarked for display with the Smithsonian Institute's National Air & Space Museum at Dulles International Airport, Washington, DC. The museum requested that the delivery flight should be a record-breaking event. To complete the feat, the aircraft departed Palmdale on March 6, crewed by Lieutenant Colonel Edward Yielding, and RSO Lieutenant Colonel Joseph T. Vida. Following a refueling near the coast of California, the crew overflew Los Angeles before setting course for Washington. In the process, the aircraft established the following speed records:

- Coast to coast; 2,404.5 statute miles in 68mins and 17secs (2,112mph)
- Los Angeles to Washington; 2,299.67 statute miles in 64mins and 5secs (2,153mph)
- Kansas City to Washington; 942.08 statute miles in 25mins and 55secs (2,181mph)
- St Louis to Cincinnati; 311.44 statute miles in 8mins and 20secs (2,242mph)

All timings were from Federal Aviation Agency radar and were verified by data from the aircraft's astro-inertial navigation system. At an altitude of 85,000ft, the speed equated to about Mach 3.2.

Amongst the remainder, 61-7976 was destined for the National Air Force Museum at Wright-Patterson AFB as the aircraft with the highest number of combat sorties. Other aircraft were flown to Palmdale where Lockheed placed them in a hangar pending their future. The SR-71 fleet was officially retired on March 6, 1990, having flown 3,551 missions during 22 years, with no aircraft lost to enemy action.

After flying numerous sorties for the USAF, and later NASA, SR-71B 831 and SR-71A 844 were in open store at Edwards for a number of years before eventually finding new homes in museums. (Andy Thomson)

NASA 844 departs Edwards during November 1998, fitted with the NASA/Lockheed Martin Linear Aerospike SR-71 Experiment (LARSE) to gather in-flight data for future reusable launch vehicles. (NASA)

Below: The LARSE being lowered gently into place aboard SR-71 NASA 844 during 1998, inside one of the huge NASA hangars. (NASA)

NASA

The premature retirement of the SR-71 by the USAF did not end Blackbird flight operations, as NASA had a requirement for high altitude research. SR-71As 61-7971 and 61-7980, along with SR-71B 61-7956, were loaned to NASA and relocated to Edwards AFB during February 1990. 61-7956, 61-7971 and 61-7980 were allocated NASA serials 831, 832 and 844, respectively. Various high altitude test programs were undertaken to evaluate experiments associated with space technology.

NASA SR-71A 832 is parked at Edwards on 23 October 1993. At the time, NASA was the sole Blackbird operator, although the US Congress was beginning to formulate the 1995 Defense Authorization Bill to restore the SR-71 to USAF service. (Chris Lofting)

Above: NASA's SR-71B making a spirited flypast at Edwards on the occasion of the final flight. (Dan Stijovich)

Left: SR-71B NASA 831 departs Edwards for the final time on October 19, 1997. At the completion of the sortie, the aircraft was retired, and eventually displayed at the Kalamazoo Air Museum in Michigan. (Dan Stijovich)

The annual open house weekend staged at Edwards AFB usually had one SR-71 on static display, with a second occasionally included in the flying program. The event staged on October 9 and 10, 1999, was planned to include SR-71A NASA 844 making a noisy departure ahead of conducting a flypast at a speed of Mach 3.21, at an altitude of 80,000ft. On the first day, the sonic boom echoed across the high desert for miles, before the jet landed and taxied past the delighted crowd to rapturous applause. 844 was due to repeat the performance on the second day, but this was canceled due to a technical issue. Therefore, the flight on October 9 was to be the final flight by an SR-71, as NASA withdrew the aircraft soon afterwards. All three aircraft were subsequently rehoused in museums, with 61-7980 being displayed by the NASA complex at Edwards AFB.

NASA 844 taking off for the final SR-71 flight at Edwards on October 9, 1999. The planned sortie the next day was canceled due to a technical problem with the aircraft. (Steve Walker collection)

NASA 844 departs Edwards accompanied by an FA-18B chase aircraft. All operational sorties were escorted by a fighter aircraft for as long as possible to film every aspect of the flight for later analysis. (NASA)

The huge sky and the flat high desert plateau dwarf NASA's SR-71A 61-7980 during an early training session at Edwards. The vast rock-hard salt flats offer a massive landing area in addition to the conventional runways. (NASA)

Big Safari

The Big Safari office, with headquarters at Wright-Patterson AFB, was not involved in the SR-71 program during the 1960s, although understandably there was a working relationship between the organization, other USAF offices, and the manufacturer. This was primarily because Senior Crown was a black program, with no direct AFLC involvement, although various AFLC departments provided indirect support, including those at Norton AFB, and AF Plant/Palmdale.

However, following the decision to reactivate the SR-71 program, Big Safari was requested to oversee the arrangements, carry out preparations, and organize operations. This was achieved under budget, as already identified, and within the stipulated timeframe. Nevertheless, while Big Safari could achieve miraculous accomplishments within its organization, it was unable to make any headway in preventing the second withdrawal process.

Following the terrorist attacks on the US on September 11, 2001, the Pentagon raised the possibility of a second SR-71 reinstatement. Big Safari made investigations, although some of the senior generals who had killed off the program four years earlier were still in post and did nothing to assist. Therefore, the retired Blackbirds remained in their museum locations, where they still reside today.

Chapter 5

Tail Art, KC-135s, T-38s, and Test vs Operations

SR-71 Tail Art

Highly classified programs seemingly attracted gifted characters within both officer and NCO ranks. These personnel sought highly inventive ways of alleviating the stress and constraints placed upon them to maintain the high level of security required. Additionally, within each group, there were always members who were imaginative artists. Their artwork was often applied in chalk, to ensure that apart from being easily cleaned, it did not degrade the paint or metal which would have potentially jeopardized the safety of the crew.

While artwork was not commonplace on SR-71s within Europe, there were many decorated aircraft at Kadena, and others at Beale towards the end of the program. There were almost four dozen artworks displayed, usually on the tails, but occasionally elsewhere. Some were quite short-lived, as the chalk soon washed off, while others were pained, and therefore remained longer. Detachment 1 at Kadena applied a red "1" to the tail, with a Habu snake coiled around. Several aircraft carried this design. Detachment 4 at Mildenhall, however, rarely applied any form of artwork, although one or two aircraft arrived with chalk inscriptions, which were soon removed. The most famous being *"The Bododian" Express*.

Many of the more permanent schemes were applied towards the end of the operational period, and began to appear on aircraft at Beale as these were to remain in the US and were therefore not exposed to missions close to adversaries' borders. The following is a known selection, although there are certain to be many more.

SR-71B 61-7956 was appropriately named *1000th Sortie* for this historic flight on January 15, 1982. The trainer aircraft achieved the most Blackbird sorties and had accumulated 3,760 flight hours before being shared with NASA. The jet remained in the US throughout its career. (via Jim Goodall)

61-7955	Black skunk on a white circle
61-7956	*1000th Sortie*
61-7956	Gumby

SR-71B 61-7956 with a Gumby drawing applied in chalk. This was possibly in 1982, as the *1000th Sortie* tail marking is almost visible, having recently been partially washed off. (Steve Walker collection)

61-7958	A white Habu snake

A white coiled Habu snake on 61-7958. (Shreeve collection)

61-7958	White Habu snake around a red "1"
61-7960	White Habu snake around a red "1"
61-7960	*Nightmare*

Carrying artwork and the name *Nightmare* on the tail, 61-7960 taxies at Beale during May 1988. (Joe Cupido)

61-7961	A bald eagle named *Bald But Bold*
61-7962	Speedy Gonzales shouting "Arriba, Arriba" and named *Numero Uno*
61-7962	Jolly Roger skull and crossbones

Skull and crossbones on the tail of 61-7962. (Shreeve collection)

61-7962	Snoopy lying on a dog kennel with fake bullet holes
61-7962	"R.I.P. Detachment 1 1968–1990"
61-7964	*"The Bododian" Express* above a crab
61-7964	"MAC & Crew" and "FOR SALE"
61-7964	Habu mission marks
61-7964	"Sky Shark"
61-7967	Yellow lightning bolt across red number "1"
61-7967	"#10" (zapped by Detachment 2)
61-7967	Red "1" with Detachment 2 emblem added, creating the number 10
61-7967	White skunk motif

Displaying a small skunk motif on the fin, 61-7967 is at Beale during September 1985. (Fred Omega)

61-7968	*DBX (Dolby Noise Reduction)* with an overflying SR-71
61-6968	*I Ain't No Cherry*
61-7970	Skateboarding Pink Panther named *Super Skater*
61-7971	*We're the Fakawee*
61-7971	Happy dog surfboarding

A happy looking dog surfs on the fin of 61-7971. (Shreeve collection)

61-7972	Detachment 4 dartboard
61-7972	*Deer Slayer*
61-7972	A pregnant Lucy with the name *Charlie's Problem*
61-7972	Black skunk on a white circle
61-7974	Habu snake wrapped around red number "1" and the inscription *Ichi Ban*
61-7974	Dennis the Menace riding a scooter
61-7974	White Charlie Brown
61-7974	Skunk emblem
61-7975	"Black Cats" (Detachment 2) logo
61-7975	White Habu snake around a red "1"
61-7976	A pregnant Lucy with a limp Habu snake named *Charlie's Problem*

A full-color Bengal tiger head is painted on 61-7976 at Beale. (David Allison)

61-7976	Bengal tiger head
61-7976	Playboy Bunny – known as *Rapid Rabbit*
61-7978	Playboy Bunny – known as *Rapid Rabbit*
61-7979	"Night Hawk"

Stylized artwork and name "Night Hawk" on 61-7979. (Shreeve collection)

61-7980	Detachment 4 dartboard
61-7980	*Rosemary's Baby-San*
61-7980	An eagle motif
61-7981	Olympia beer can

Detachment 2 at Edwards AFB had the red "BB" stenciled on its aircraft. NASA aircraft had its old-style logo, as well as the later "Worm" insignia on the tail. Other artwork and inscriptions were applied to the main landing gear doors, along with small Habu snake symbols aft of the cockpit following sorties flown from Kadena. Several aircraft displayed the 9th SRW emblem on the fin, including 61-7958, 61-7960, 61-7963, 61-7976 and 61-7979.

Above left: Early SR-71 missions from Kadena to overfly North Vietnam were commemorated by ground crews with a white Habu sprayed onto an area aft of the cockpit. The aircraft in question, with 43 missions displayed, is probably 61-7974. (via Jim Goodall)

Above right: Until the introduction of low visibility red markings, several aircraft had the full color Wing emblem applied to the tails. (via Jim Goodall)

Above left One of the few SR-71s that did not rotate to the UK, 61-7963 flew operationally from Kadena before being display at Beale's Heritage Park. (Steve Walker collection)

Above right The Dolby Noise Reduction logo was applied to the tail of 61-7968 at Kadena sometime between July 1985 and May 1987. (via Jim Goodall)

Above left: Most artwork was confined to a single subject and reasonably small. However, that applied to 61-7972 sometime prior to 1982 is extremely garish, with many ground crew seemingly let loose to vent their feelings upon the hapless Blackbird. (via Jim Goodall)

Above right: As the days of SR-71 operations began to appear numbered, there was an increasing growth of artwork being applied to aircraft at Beale. During May 1988, 61-7960 was displaying a caricature of a fox's head and the name *Nightmare*. (Joe Cupido)

Above left: Small tail marking of an Olympia beer can on SR-71C 61-7981. (via Jim Goodall)

Above right: No aircraft were ever flown from Mildenhall with the Detachment 4 dartboard applied. However, 61-7980 featured this marking during the early period of loan to NASA. (Jim Goodall)

Skull and crossbones were a popular decoration for military hardware, with SR-71A 61-7962 displaying them at Kadena sometime after 1983. (David Allison)

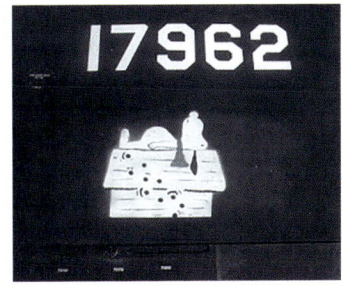

Above left: 61-7970 with a panther on a skateboard named *Super Skater* during a Kadena deployment. (via Jim Goodall)

Above middle: Interesting tail art on 61-7961 composed of a US bald eagle and the legend *Bald But Bold*. (via Jim Goodall)

Above right: Snoopy lying on his dog kennel has appeared on several different aircraft types, including SR-71A 61-7962. (via Jim Goodall)

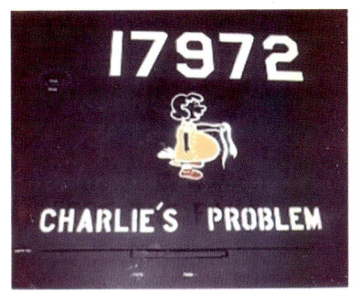

Above left: 61-7962 had Speedy Gonzales shouting "Arriba, Arriba," and the name *Numero Uno*. (via Jim Goodall)

Above middle: 61-7971 was named *W'ere The Fakawee*. This is a rude play on words, about a group of native Red Indians who wandered the forest for a long time, lost. One shouted "W'ere The Fakawee," in the hope that someone would hear, and come to their rescue! (via Jim Goodall)

Above right: More than one SR-71 displayed a pregnant Lucy (from the *Peanuts* cartoon series) with the name *Charlie's Problem*. (via Jim Goodall)

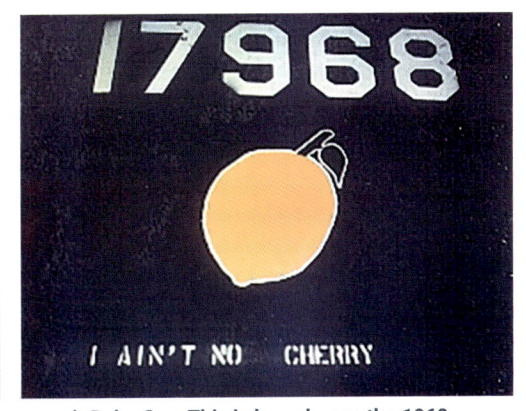

Above left: 61-7980 depicting a baby devil, and the name *Rosemary's Baby-San*. This is based upon the 1968 movie of the same name, but with the Japanese word "San" added. San is an honorific title used to address someone with a higher status in a respectful and polite way. (via Jim Goodall)

Above right: 61-7968 with a peach and the legend *I Ain't No Cherry*. (via Jim Goodall)

Boeing KC-135A and KC-135Q

Throughout the life of the Blackbird series, specially configured KC-135s provided the necessary aerial refueling. Prior to the delivery of the first A-12s to the CIA, SAC's 4126th SW was formed at Beale on February 8, 1959, and received its first KC-135A beginning on July 14, 1959, when 58-0074 joined the unit. A further eight were received by June 1, 1960, with six more transferred from other SAC units soon afterwards, assigned to the 903rd Air Refueling Squadron (AREFS). The squadron was selected to provide dedicated support to the Blackbirds located initially at Area 51, as Beale was only 300 miles from the Nevada base. Furthermore, Beale was identified as the likely station for Blackbird operations, if and when these were assigned to the USAF – which they eventually were.

The 4126th was replaced by the 456th Strategic Aerospace Wing (later Bomb Wing, BW) at Beale on February 1, 1963, until September 30, 1975, when the 17th BW was the primary tanker unit at the base. In turn, the 17th BW was inactivated on September 30, 1976, with the tankers assigned direct to the 9th SRW. The 100th ARW was activated to administer the tankers on September 1976, until inactivated on March 15, 1983, when the KC-135s were again assigned directly to the 9th SRW. The 903rd AREFS was the sole tanker squadron until January 1, 1970, when the 9th AREFS formed. Both the 9th and 903rd AREFSs were in residence until they inactivated on January 28, 1982, and September 30, 1976, respectively. They were replaced by the 349th and 350th AREFSs on September 30, 1976, and January 28, 1982, respectively.

58-0074 was the first KC-135A delivered to Beale, arriving on July 14, 1959, for assignment to the 4126th Strategic Wing. The unit was replaced by the 456th Strategic Aerospace Wing in 1963, with 58-0074 subsequently being redesignated as a KC-135Q on September 8, 1967. It is parked at Mildenhall on August 4, 1973, although with no SR-71 operations in Europe the tanker was flying conventional sorties at the time. (Bob Archer)

A rare image of KC-135Q 60-0342 at Mildenhall on April 18, 1976, assigned to the 17th Bomb Wing. The unit was responsible for the Beale tankers for only one year, before being replaced by the 100th ARW. (Bob Archer)

The SR-71s became operational at Beale AFB at the same time the A-12s were retired. Initially the KC-135As refueled the Blackbirds with the specialized JP-7 fuel housed in the normal tanks, which were cleansed with an air flush before reverting to conventional tanker missions. The 903rd AREFS briefly supported the SR-71 in this manner, although it soon became apparent that the KC-135As needed separate tanks, as well as secure communications to ensure effective interactions.

A total of 56 tankers were upgraded during the first half of 1967, returning to service between May 31 and November 1. Half of the conversions were delivered to Beale. Modified tankers were designated as the KC-135Q, with individual fuel tanks for JP-7 filled through a separate ground refueling receptacle. Furthermore, a third UHF radio was installed as well as a tactical air navigation system. The extra UHF radio provided distance measurement between the tanker and the Blackbird, enabling highly accurate navigation without the need for voice communication.

After the 100th ARW was replaced by the 9th SRW at Beale, the KC-135Qs adopted the distinctive four Maltese/iron crosses on a yellow tail stripe. 58-0062 landing at Mildenhall on April 26, 1985. (Bob Archer)

For the entire period of Mildenhall operations, the KC-135Qs were powered by the Pratt & Whitney J57 jet engines, which required water injection to produce steam and augment their take-off roll. The practice was noisy and produced a great deal of pollution. KC-135Q 58-0084 demonstrates this procedure at Mildenhall on January 9, 1989. (Bob Archer)

The tankers retained the conventional SAC markings, being largely anonymous apart from the Wing emblem located starboard side of the "milky way" fuselage sash. When SAC introduced tail stripes, the 9th SRW adopted a yellow band containing four black Maltese crosses. Subsequently, the tankers were camouflaged, retaining the same tail design but in low-visibility format. Tail code "BB" was applied when SAC was inactivated, and the tankers were reassigned to ACC on June 1, 1992. However, when ACC relinquished the aerial refueling role to Air Mobility Command on September 30, 1993, the tankers changed to a pale blue fin stripe with "BEALE" in black letters. This was retained until 1994, when the two squadrons were relocated to McConnell AFB, Missouri, with the 22nd ARW.

Left: For decades, the T-38A faithfully served the Blackbird community, providing senior commanders with the necessary ability to evaluate potential pilots during the selection process. (Dan Stijovich)

Below: 9th RW T-38A 64-13301 flying off the California coast during a training sortie. It is commonplace for aircrew to fly cross-country sorties, with 9th T-38s often seen in popular areas at weekends. (USAF)

Northrop T-38A Talon

Before being selected to become one of the small cadre of elite Blackbird aircrew, pilots and RSOs were assessed during a minimum of two flights in a T-38A, accompanied by the squadron commander or a senior crew member. The T-38 was considered a companion trainer, enabling proficiency flying at a fraction of the cost of a Blackbird.

Initially, the T-38s were operated in the anonymous gloss-white color scheme of Air Training Command. Not long afterwards, these were enhanced with the SAC emblem on the tail, and, shortly after, the 9th SRW yellow tail stripe containing four black crosses. Later, the gloss black overall scheme was adopted with a red tail stripe containing the four crosses. Tail code "BB" was also adopted when the Wing transferred from SAC to ACC. Approximately a dozen T-38s were assigned, and most remain current at Beale, as the Talon now supports the U-2 program.

After years of being painted white overall, with the yellow and black unit markings, all the Beale-based T-38As changed to a gloss black overall scheme, the same as those of Air Education and Training Command. Unit insignia was applied in red. (Louis DePaemelaere)

64-13281 of the 9th SRW visiting NAS Dallas, Texas, in January 1982. Early T-38 assignments simply displayed the command emblem on the fin, with the yellow stripes added later. (Peter Wilson)

Apart from the T-38As, which were stationed at Beale to support the SR-71s, at least two others were assigned Air Force Logistics Command (AFLC) duties associated with the Blackbird. Former NASA Talon 63-8204 was being flown by Detachment 51, 2762th Logistics Squadron (Support), at Palmdale when visiting McChord AFB, Washington, during June 1975. [Doug Remington]

At least two more T-38As were associated with the SR-71. They were stationed at Palmdale with Detachment 51, to act as chase aircraft during SR-71 test flights. 65-10363 was white overall, with a thick dark blue cheatline and fin tip. An SR-71 silhouette was applied to the tail. The second was 63-8204, which also had the thick blue cheat line, but with a broad yellow band across the tail containing an SR-71 silhouette. Both were previously with NASA and are believed to have reverted to the Administration when the SR-71 program was deactivated.

Above: Another AFLC T-38A 65-10363 with the stylized tail band of Detachment 6, 2762nd Logistics Squadron (Support) at Palmdale, visiting Davis-Monthan AFB during May 1981. (Ben Knowles)

Left: 9th RW commander's 64-13271 at Beale on June 10, 1999, shortly before the Blackbird program was axed for the second time. (Brian Rogers)

Below: 9th RW T-38A 64-13240 flying low level through the canyons in Arizona. (Chris Woods)

Test vs operational

As stated earlier, the first six aircraft, 61-7950 to 61-7955, were ordered for evaluation and development, followed by the aircraft numbers seven and eight, 61-7956 and 61-7957, constructed for the training role. The next 23, 61-7958 to 61-7980, were built for operations, and were configured differently from the test versions. The remaining example, 61-7981, was a hybrid trainer, constructed later from two halves of others involved in accidents or retired.

Of the 23 intended for operations, 18 deployed to Kadena, while 13 were at Mildenhall. Aircraft that flew from Kadena, but not Mildenhall, were 61-7961, 61-7963, 61-7968, 61-7969, 61-7970, and 61-7978, while only 61-7973 deployed to the UK, but not Okinawa. Operational aircraft that served neither location were 61-7959, 61-7965, 61-7966 and 61-7977. The latter three were lost in accidents prior to being selected to perform overseas missions. 61-7959 was also devoted to test duties, evaluating aft-facing electronic countermeasures in an extended fairing, beginning on December 3, 1975. Despite being operationally configured, this aircraft did not perform any overseas deployments, and was retired in October 1976 at the completion of trials. The only test jet that was operated overseas was 61-7955 from Mildenhall, detailed elsewhere. Twelve SR-71s were lost to accidents; four test aircraft and eight operational versions.

Having completed deliveries, Lockheed retained at least one SR-71 for ongoing development work. 61-7955 was the primary jet involved, and it was occasionally statically displayed at air shows in California, particularly at Norton AFB, which was involved in the Blackbird supply chain. The aircraft displayed a white circle containing a black skunk. The aircraft was withdrawn during January 1985.

The hybrid trainer, SR-71C 61-7981, was known by several nicknames, some of which were unflattering, as the jet was produced from surplus airframes and components. Seen at Beale during January 1981. (Hugh Muir)

Lockheed SR-71 Blackbird

Above left: Throughout the majority of its flying career, 61-7955 carried the famous Lockheed skunk emblem on the tail. When retired in January 1985, 61-7974 and 61-7972 were two that continued the development work and continued to display this decoration. (Bob Archer)

Above right: When 61-7955 was retired in January 1985, AFLC received 61-7972 as a replacement. As the aircraft was retained in the US for development work, the command emblem was applied in red, along with a full color skunk motif. (via Jim Goodall)

Left: Former operational SR-71s were periodically assigned to the Lockheed's Skunk Works for development work. 61-7974 displays the skunk emblem sometime during the 1970s. (via Jim Goodall)

   Two other aircraft are known to have been allocated to Lockheed for a similar role. 61-7974 displayed the white disc and skunk emblem during the period when the aircraft had the serial presented in white, which was during the 1970s. This would have been sometime after June 1971, when the aircraft completed a deployment to Kadena, and July 1982, when '974 commenced assignment to Detachment 4. The third aircraft was 61-7972, which also displayed the white disc and skunk on the tail. However, the serial was in red, so it was placed after 1983. As '955 ceased flying in 1985, it was quite probably after this time. 61-7972 also had the AFLC emblem in red, as this was the link element between Lockheed and the USAF.

Skunk Works SR-71A 61-7972 landing at March AFB during October 1982. Note the low visibility serial, which was possibly one of the first to feature the toned-down markings. (Dan Stijovich)

Appendix 1
SR-71 Deployments to Detachment 1 and 4

The two overseas Detachment locations for SR-71 missions flew 18 different aircraft at Kadena, and 14 from Mildenhall. Kadena began operations in March 1968, while the first to stage to Mildenhall was six years later in September 1974.

Detachment 1

Serial number	Deployment date	Redeployment date
61-7958	July 17, 1980 (H)	July 16, 1981 (H)
61-7960	August 10, 1977 (H)	June 23, 1979 (H)
	September 4, 1980 (H)	July 15, 1981(H)
	November 12, 1983 (H)	November 20, 1983
61-7961	August 18, 1972	June 7, 1973
	August 16, 1974	July 21, 1976
61-7962	September 18, 1968	April 25, 1969
	June 6, 1973	August 20, 1974
	June 22, 1979 (H)	June 24, 1980 (H)
	June 9, 1989 (H)	January 21, 1990 (Last out)
61-7963	August 21, 1972	June 13, 1973
	August 13, 1974	July 16, 1976
61-7964	February 15, 1983 (H)	March 30, 1984 (H)
	December 11, 1984 (H)	August 1, 1985 (H)
61-7967	August 14, 1977	August 3, 1979
	July 16, 1981 (H)	June 30, 1982
	April 4, 1986 (H)	November 20, 1987 (H)
61-7968	June 19, 1971	August 19, 1972
	June 12, 1973	August 14, 1974
	July 31, 1985 (H)	May 14, 1987 (H)
61-7969	September 24, 1969	May 10, 1970 (Crashed in Thailand)
61-7970	September 15, 1968	April 22, 1969

Serial number	Deployment date	Redeployment date
61-7971	April 18, 1969	October 1, 1969
	August 14, 1972	June 10, 1973
	November 26, 1974	July 14, 1976
61-7972	September 30, 1969	June 11, 1971
	June 9, 1973	August 17, 1974
	July 17, 1976	August 11, 1977 (H)
61-7974	March 13, 1968	September 16, 1968
	October 3, 1969	June 14, 1971
	November 19, 1987 (H)	April 21, 1989 (Crashed in the Philippine Sea)

61-7974 at Kadena in July 1988, after the application of toned-down markings. (Masanori Ogawa)

61-7975	April 24, 1969	October 22, 1969
	December 18, 1970	June 17, 1971
	August 12, 1977	July 20, 1979 (H)
	July 14, 1980 (H)	February 17, 1983 (H)
	May 13, 1987 (H)	June 30, 1988 (H)
61-7976	March 11, 1968	September 13, 1968
	August 19, 1974	January 30, 1975
	July 20, 1976	August 9, 1977
	June 24, 1980 (H)	June 7, 1982
	November 19, 1983 (H)	December 13, 1984 (H)

Serial number	Deployment date	Redeployment date
61-7978	March 9, 1968	September 19, 1968
	June 16, 1971	July 20, 1972 (Written off at Kadena)
61-7979	April 21, 1968	September 25, 1969
	June 13, 1971	August 12, 1972
	July 13, 1976	August 13, 1977
	August 2, 1979 (H)	September 5, 1980 (H)
	July 3, 1988 (H)	August 12, 1988 (H)
61-7980	September 12, 1968	April 19, 1969
	June 19, 1971	August 15, 1972
	June 6, 1982	November 13, 1982 (H)

Note: (H) = Habu Operational flight conducted en route between the US and Kadena. The first SR-71 to incorporate an operational mission during its redeployment flight profile from Kadena to Beale was flown by Al Cirino and Bruce Liebman in serial 61-7976 on August 9, 1977. The next day, Maury Rosenberg and Al Payne arrived at Kadena in serial 61-7960, having successfully completed the first operational sortie en route to Kadena from Beale.

Taxiing to a parking area after the lengthy flight from Beale, SR-71A 61-7979 is at Mildenhall on April 17, 1979. (Paul Bennett)

Detachment 4

Serial number	Deployment date	Redeployment date
61-7972	September 9, 1974	September 13, 1974
61-7972	April 20, 1976	April 30, 1976
61-7962	September 6, 1976	September 18, 1976
61-7958	January 7, 1977	January 17, 1977
61-7958	May 16, 1977	May 31, 1977
61-7976	October 24, 1977	November 16, 1977
61-7964	April 24, 1978	May 12, 1978
61-7964	October 16, 1978	November 2, 1978
61-7972	March 12, 1979	March 28, 1979
61-7979	April 17, 1979	May 2, 1979
61-7976	October 18, 1979	November 13, 1979
61-7976	April 4, 1980	May 9, 1980
61-7972	September 13, 1980	November 2, 1980
61-7964	December 12, 1980	March 7, 1981
61-7972	March 6, 1981	May 5, 1981

The majority of visits to Mildenhall by 61-7972 were during the early period of operations. The aircraft is seen taxiing past the Team Mildenhall hangar on April 18, 1981. (Don Gilham)

61-7964	August 16, 1981 (From Bodo)	November 6, 1981
61-7958	December 16, 1981	December 21, 1981
61-7980	January 5, 1982	April 27, 1982
61-7974	April 30, 1982	December 13, 1982
61-7972	December 18, 1982	July 6, 1983

Serial number	Deployment date	Redeployment date
61-7971	December 23, 1982	February 2, 1983
61-7980	March 7, 1983	September 6, 1983
61-7955	July 9, 1983	July 30, 1983 (with false serial 17962)
61-7974	August 2, 1983	July 16, 1984
61-7958	September 9, 1983	June 12, 1984
61-7979	June 14, 1984	July 17, 1985
61-7975	July 16, 1984	October 16, 1984
61-7962	October 19, 1984	October 23, 1985
61-7980	July 19, 1985	October 29, 1986
61-7960	October 29, 1985	January 29, 1987
61-7973	November 1, 1986	July 22, 1987
61-7964	February 5, 1987	March 3, 1988
61-7980	July 27, 1987	October 3, 1988 (From Lakenheath)
61-7971	March 13, 1988	February 28, 1989
61-7964	October 5, 1988 (To Lakenheath)	January 18, 1990*
61-7967	March 2, 1989	January 19, 1990

* This aircraft completed an operational mission into the Barents Sea after a flyby at Mildenhall upon its departure, despite the fact that the program had been terminated the previous November. Details of other flights between Beale and Mildenhall, which incorporated an operation to the traditional target areas, have not been made available. However, almost all of these Busy Relay sorties included an intelligence gathering element.

After spending its entire career conducting development work with Lockheed, 61-7955 was flown from Palmdale to Edwards on January 24, 1985, to be officially retired. After a period of storage at Edwards, the aircraft was eventually allocated to the Air Force Flight Test Center's museum and placed alongside other future exhibits. It is seen at Edwards on October 21, 2000. (Bob Archer)

Appendix 2
First and Last Flights

Manufacturers ordinarily record details of the delivery date for all new aircraft. However, the Blackbirds were different, as they did not conduct a maiden flight at a similar time to being accepted into the inventory. Instead, they were accepted and trucked by road to either Area 51 or Palmdale for final assembly and their first flight. Therefore, the three Blackbird types only record details of the first and last flight, and in several cases, this information remains unknown.

Serial	First Flight	Last Flight	Subsequent
SR-71			
61-7950	December 23, 1964	January 10, 1967	Crashed
61-7951	March 5, 1965	December 22, 1978	Pima Air Museum, AZ
61-7952	March 24, 1965	January 25, 1966	Crashed
61-7953	June 4, 1965	December 18, 1969	Crashed
61-7954	July 20, 1965	April 11, 1969	Crashed
61-7955	August 17, 1965	January 24, 1985	AFFTC Museum, Edwards AFB, CA
61-7956	August 17, 1965	October 19, 1997	Kalamazoo Air Museum, MI

Flying days completed, SR-71B 831 taxies to park for the last time on October 19, 1997. (Andy Thomson)

Serial	First Flight	Last Flight	Subsequent
61-7957	December 18, 1965	January 11, 1968	Crashed
61-7958	December 15, 1965	February 23, 1990	Museum of Aviation, Robins, GA

61-7958 was flown from Beale to Robins AFB, Georgia, on February 23, 1990, and following the removal of fuel was towed the short distance to the Museum of Aviation. (The tow vehicle appears very similar to the electric car nicknamed "Jeff," which James May designed for a challenge on *Top Gear*.) (Museum of Aviation)

Serial	First Flight	Last Flight	Subsequent
61-7959	January 19, 1966	October 29, 1976	AF Armament Museum, Eglin AFB, FL
61-7960	February 9, 1966	February 27, 1990	Castle Air Museum, CA
61-7961	April 13, 1966	February 2, 1977	Cosmosphere, Hutchinson, KS
61-7962	April 29, 1966	February 14, 1990	IWM, Duxford, UK

A rare outing for Duxford's SR-71A 61-7962 during September 2015 when the large American Air Museum was emptied of exhibits to carry out safety inspections. (Bob Archer)

Serial	First Flight	Last Flight	Subsequent
61-7963	June 9, 1966	October 28, 1976	Beale AFB, CA
61-7964	May 11, 1966	March 20, 1990	Strategic Air Command & Space Museum, Ashland, NE
61-7965	June 10, 1966	October 25, 1967	Crashed
61-7966	July 1, 1966	April 13, 1967	Crashed
61-7967	August 3, 1966	February 14, 1990	
	to NASA	9 May 1996	Barksdale AFB, LA
61-7968	August 3, 1966	February 12, 1990	Virginia Aviation Museum, Richmond, VA
61-7969	October 18, 1966	May 10, 1970	Crashed
61-7970	October 21, 1966	June 17, 1970	Crashed
61-7971	November 17, 1966	June 14, 1996	Evergreen Air Museum, McMinnville, OR
61-7972	December 12, 1966	March 6, 1990	Smithsonian, Washington, DC
61-7973	February 8, 1967	July 22, 1987	Blackbird Airpark, Palmdale, CA
61-7974	February 16, 1967	April 21, 1989	Crashed
61-7975	April 13, 1967	February 28, 1990	March Field, CA
61-7976	May 1967	March 27, 1990	National Museum of the USAF, Wright-Patterson AFB, OH
61-7977	Unknown	October 10, 1968	Crashed
61-7978	Unknown	July 20, 1972	Crashed
61-7979	August 10, 1967	March 6, 1990	Lackland AFB, TX
61-7980	September 25, 1967	February 5, 1990	
	to NASA	October 9, 1999	NASA Dryden, Edwards AFB, CA
61-7981	March 14, 1969	April 11, 1976	Hill AFB, UT

Photographed during the spring of 1990, shortly after transfer to NASA, 61-7980 is seen with the Detachment 4 dartboard emblem on the fin. (NASA)

A-12

Serial	First Flight	Last Flight	Subsequent
60-6924	April 28, 1962	Unknown	Blackbird Air Park, Palmdale CA
60-6925	Unknown	Unknown	USS *Intrepid*, New York, NY
60-6926	October 1962	May 24, 1963	Crashed
60-6927	January 22, 1963	Unknown	Los Angeles, CA
60-6928	January 1963	January 5, 1967	Crashed
60-6929	March 1963	December 28, 1967	Crashed
60-6930	March 1963	Unknown	Huntsville, AL
60-6931	June 1963	January 5, 1967	HQ CIA, Langley, VA
60-6932	Unknown	June 5, 1968	Crashed
60-6933	November 27, 1963	August 1965	San Diego, CA
60-6937	February 19, 1964	June 21, 1968	Birmingham, AL
60-6938	Unknown	January 5, 1967	USS *Alabama*, Mobile, AL
60-6939	March 18, 1964	July 9, 1964	Crashed
60-6940	Unknown	Unknown	Seattle, WA
60-6941	Unknown	May 30, 1966	Crashed

The YF-12s were a regular feature of the 1960s Edwards annual open days. 60-6936 taxies at the base on May 22, 1966. (Don Larsen)

Early image of YF-12A 60-6934 in natural metal finish and appearing to have the serial and buzz number applied with an adhesive decal. The buzz number system was in vogue during the first half of the 1960s, with "FX" allocated to the proposed air defense Blackbird version. (Lockheed)

Serial	First Flight	Last Flight	Subsequent
YF-12A			
60-6934	August 8, 1963	August 14, 1966	To SR-71C 61-7981
60-6935	November 26, 1963	November 7, 1979	USAFM Wright-Patterson AFB, OH
60-6936	March 13, 1964	July 24, 1971	Crashed

YF-12A 60-6935 joined the National Museum of the USAF at Wright-Patterson AFB, Ohio, on November 7, 1979. (Dave Menard)

The white YF-12 mission symbols were applied to the nose of 60-6936 during May 1970. Despite proving extremely effective against airborne targets, Defense Secretary McNamara instituted protracted procurement delays, thereby protecting funds for the North American XB-70 and the prospective F-106X program. (via Jim Goodall)

Serial	First Flight	Last Flight	Subsequent
YF-12C			
60-6937	July 16, 1971	October 27, 1978	Reverted to 61-7951

61-7967 taxiing for a training mission at Mildenhall during June 1989. Despite being extremely expensive to operate, aircrew were required to carry out overseas training flights periodically to ensure they were proficient during operational sorties. (Bob Archer)

SR-71A 61-7975 was flown from Beale to March AFB on February 28, 1990, to join the Air Museum. A ceremony was staged to welcome the aircraft and crew, with the museum's U-2, joined by a resident KC-10A and a KC-135A and a support T-38A. (USAF)

SR-71A 61-7960 taxies from its barn at Beale during April 1984. (Joe Cupido)

Above left: A commemorative patch for 61-7958 being delivered to Robins AFB on February 23, 1990. (Bob Archer collection)

Above right: A patch for the final flight of 61-7960, which was flown at the retirement ceremony at Beale in January 1990. Despite suggesting the aircraft was flown to Castle Museum that day, the aircraft did not arrive for display until one month later. (Bob Archer collection)

Above left: The patch to celebrate 61-7972 performing a record-breaking flight from coast to coast to land at Dulles, Washington, DC, on March 6, 1990. (Bob Archer collection)

Above right: The flight by 61-7975 on February 28, 1990, to March AFB was highlighted on a patch. (Bob Archer collection)

Above left: A patch commemorating 61-7976 taking the final Blackbird flight on March 27, 1990, to Dayton. Subsequently, the type flew with NASA, and was five years later reintroduced to USAF service, although the reinstatement was not known at the time. (Bob Archer collection)

Above right: The sixth and last patch was for 61-7979 flying to Lackland AFB on March 6, 1990. (Bob Archer collection)

An extremely sad occasion when 61-7964 taxied from the safety of the individual barn on January 18, 1990, for the last time. 61-7964 enjoyed an exciting career, with interesting diversions, as well as six deployments to Detachment 4 at Mildenhall. The jet is now displayed with the Strategic Air Command & Space Museum at Ashland, Nebraska. (Bob Archer)

Other books you might like:

LOCKHEED C-141 STARLIFTER
BOB ARCHER
Historic Military Aircraft Series, Vol. 9

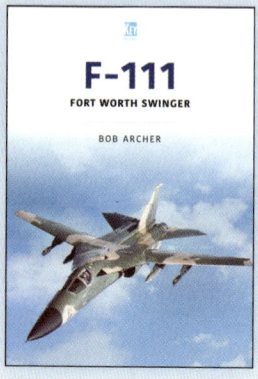

F-111 FORT WORTH SWINGER
BOB ARCHER
Historic Military Aircraft Series, Vol. 3

LOCKHEED CONSTELLATION
Historic Commercial Aircraft Series, Vol. 8

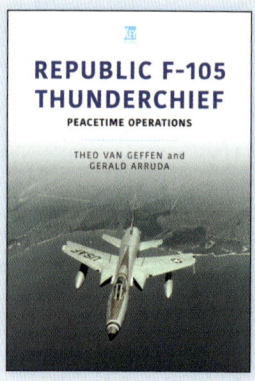

REPUBLIC F-105 THUNDERCHIEF PEACETIME OPERATIONS
THEO VAN GEFFEN and GERALD ARRUDA
Historic Military Aircraft Series, Vol. 6

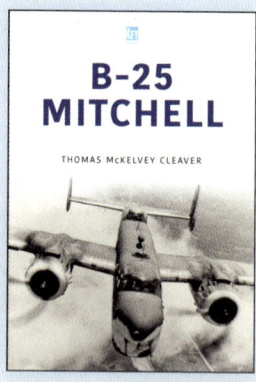

B-25 MITCHELL
THOMAS McKELVEY CLEAVER
Historic Military Aircraft Series, Vol. 12

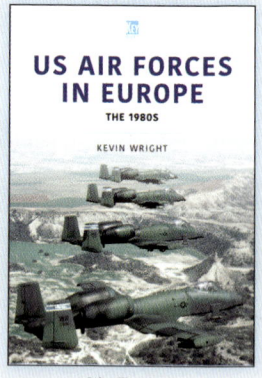

US AIR FORCES IN EUROPE THE 1980S
KEVIN WRIGHT
Air Forces Series, Vol. 4

For our full range of titles please visit:
shop.keypublishing.com/books

VIP Book Club

Sign up today and receive
TWO FREE E-BOOKS

Be the first to find out about our forthcoming book releases and receive exclusive offers.

Register now at **keypublishing.com/vip-book-club**

Our VIP Book Club is a 100% spam-free zone, and we will never share your email with anyone else. You can read our full privacy policy at: privacy.keypublishing.com